LIGHTFOOD

Eating for Consciousness & Enlightenment

EDWARD ESKO

IMI Press
Lenox, Massachusetts

Design: ebookpbook
Cover: Wreath with cereals—barley, wheat, rye, rice, millet, and oat
By Yekaterina Nikolayenko

ISBN: 9781686199691

Published by IMI Press
P.O. Box 2051
Lenox, MA 01240

InternationalMacrobioticInstitute.com
(413) 446-2620
edwardesko@gmail.com

First edition: June 2021

PLANT × 1   PANICLES LIFE SIZE   DETAILS × 2
1 RICE plant   2 Flowering spikelet detail
3 Panicle of ripe grain   4 Panicle of awned variety
5 Details of spikelets and polished grains

9

Illustration of the rice plant. Awned rice is shown at left (numbers 1 and 4)

Naomi Ichikawa Esko with homegrown awned rice

CONTENTS

Edward Esko

The author meditating among terraced rice paddies in Nagano, Japan

INTRODUCTION

One of the most profound experiences I have had took place more than forty years ago on a clear October day in the mountains and rice fields that surround the city of Kyoto in Japan. During an afternoon walk on the outskirts of the city, I decided to stray from the main road onto one of the paths that led to a large clearing at the foot of a mountain. The plain was overflowing with fields of ripening rice, and as I continued walking, I found myself surrounded on all sides by acre after acre of golden grain. The sun was shining in a warm, late afternoon yellow and the sky was a crystal blue. The pine-studded mountains off in the distance were a brilliant green. In that beautiful natural setting, everything seemed in perfect harmony—living, breathing, vibrant with the energy of heaven and Earth. Underlying the feeling of peace, harmony, and serenity, which seemed to extend throughout the universe, was the deep sense of attraction and oneness I felt for the ripening rice. The magnetism that I experienced so vividly that afternoon is a result of the natural attraction that human beings have for the vegetable kingdom, especially cereal grains. Without such attraction, we literally would not exist, since without primary foods, there would be no life.

My next encounter with rice in the field took place in northern California, in the Sacramento Valley. Here, unlike in Japan where the average rice paddy is the size of a tennis court, the rice fields are vast and extend for what seemed like miles in all directions. It was the early 2000s, and my associates and I were in California to network with organic growers opposed to the introduction of genetically modified (GM) rice in their state. At that time, and up to the present, the Sacramento Valley served as the epicenter of organic rice farming in America. The Sacramento Valley lies at the northern rim of California's Central Valley. Rivers and streams flow from the high Sierras into the valley and provide water for the growing of crops, including rice. I described my visit in a 2001 article in the Amberwaves newsletter:

The Visitor's Center at Lake Oroville sits high above the Sacramento Valley in the foothills of the Sierras. Like most days in the Valley, the weather is clear, sunny, and warm. Perfect for growing rice. The Sacramento Valley, which stretches off toward the West, is the leading producer of organic brown rice in the United States. Alex Jack, founder of the Amber Waves Network (AWN) and I stand on the upper deck of the observation tower and trace the pattern of rivers flowing down from the Sierras. The panorama is breathtaking. A hawk glides effortlessly, high above the valley floor. Streams and rivers flow steadily downward from the high mountains. Their energy gathers several hundred feet below us in Lake Oroville. Lake Oroville was created following construction of Oroville Dam in 1968. Made of soil, the dam rises seven hundred feet above the bed of the Feather River. Rice cultivation requires a steady supply of water. Lake Oroville is the source of water for the rice fields in the Sacramento Valley.

Sandwiched between the Pacific Ocean and the Pacific Coastal Range to the West, and the Sierra Nevada to the East, the Sacramento Valley is charged by natural energy. To the North lie Mount Shasta and the Cascades. Mountain ranges are the Earth's energy meridians. They are formed by the upward push of energy generated by the Earth's rotation. Rivers are ley lines that channel energy from the mountains. Farmers in the Sacramento Valley further channel this energy through a vast network of canals that crisscross the valley and irrigate the rice fields. The successful channeling of this mountain energy has made California an agricultural powerhouse, both for conventional and organic farming.

The reason for my visit to California is to meet with organic rice farmers to discuss the status of genetically altered rice. Alex Jack and I are planning to meet with Grant Lundberg, the C.E.O. of Lundberg Family Farms. The Lundberg family has been growing rice since 1937. Today, Lundberg Farms is the largest distributor of organic brown rice in the United States. There are currently a dozen varieties of genetically modified (GM) rice in development around the world. If GM rice comes into the Sacramento Valley, there is a danger of genetic pollution caused by GM pollen drifting into the organic fields and contaminating the organic crop. America could lose its primary source of organic brown rice. Heirloom rice that has nourished humanity for thousands of years could conceivably vanish. Like wheat, barley, and the other cereal grains, rice is at the center of the human evolutionary spiral. Fifty-one percent of the world's population consumes rice as daily staple. Grains are the cornerstone of our agriculture, diet, and civilization. The genetic engineering of such an essential food could have negative implications for our entire planet.

On the following day, we set out for our meeting. On the drive from Oroville to Richvale, the home of Lundberg Farms, there are rice fields as far as the eye can see. Off in the distance are metal silos used for storing the rice crop. It is early summer, and the rice resembles tall green grass. Surrounding the fields are irrigation ditches in which cattails grow. Dragonflies swarm above. The ecology is that of a freshwater marsh. Upon arriving at Lundberg Farms, we locate Grant Lundberg's office in a small shed next to the main office building. After shaking hands, Grant leads us into his office. We begin by introducing ourselves and thanking the Lundbergs for their pioneering efforts in developing and promoting organic rice. Alex then presents a scenario in which a dozen varieties of GM rice are introduced around the world. Grant is well aware of the plans for GM rice.

The biotech industry has ambitious plans for California rice. Their hope is to see 40% of the California crop be GM by 2010. The first two varieties of GM rice set for introduction in California are the herbicide tolerant varieties "Liberty Link," developed by AgrEvo, and "Roundup Ready," developed by Monsanto. This herbicide tolerant rice is genetically engineered to accept high levels of "Liberty," the herbicide marketed by AgrEvo, and "Roundup," the herbicide marketed by Monsanto.

Grant then contrasts the Lundberg method of organic weed control with the use of Roundup and other toxic herbicides. During the summer, the Lundbergs drain the water from their organic fields. The bright sun shines down on both weeds and rice plants. The weeds dry up but the rice flourishes. The fields are again flooded and the rice continues growing without competing weeds. The Lundbergs practice a totally natural method of weed control.

Several days later, after returning to Massachusetts, I notice the latest edition of *Time* Magazine. The cover features a photo of a Swiss Professor named Ingo Potrykus with his beta-carotene-enriched rice. The headline states, "This Rice Could Save a Million Kids a Year.... but protesters believe such genetically modified foods are bad for us and our planet." So-called "golden rice," an unnatural transgenic "food," contains beta-carotene producing genes from daffodils and a certain type of bacteria. For many years, Potrykus has been waging a one-man campaign against brown rice; claiming it is nutritionally deficient. However, beta-carotene is present in the outer coat of brown rice; the part that is removed when it is milled into white rice. Most of the nutritional deficiencies in underdeveloped countries occur because people eat white, rather than brown rice, and not enough green leafy and orange-yellow vegetables. Scientists such as Potrykus begin from a false premise. They believe nature is imperfect and can be improved upon. Such blindness inevitably leads to downfall. Nature is and always will be a perfect system. However, in the case of "golden rice," this blindness is being presented under a humanitarian guise. I hope people are not fooled.

Rice farming in the Sacramento Valley has been going on for over a hundred years. GMOs are simply not needed; they interfere with the natural order and make things unnecessarily complicated. They are more of a problem than a solution. There are far better solutions to hunger and malnutrition than genetic engineering. GMOs divert attention from the root cause of these problems and make finding solutions more difficult.

Organic rice field in the Sacramento Valley

Nature operates according to the principle of "one grain, ten-thousand grains." For every seed the Earth receives, it returns thousands. Nature is forever productive, and infinitely diverse. In the practice of genetic engineering, ten thousand seeds are sacrificed for every one that comes to market, or "from ten-thousand grains, come one grain." That is the opposite of the order of nature. Originally, the heirloom seeds that sustained humanity over the centuries cost nothing; they were given freely by nature. Each genetically engineered seed costs $300 million to bring to market. We now face a choice between two opposite views of life, one natural, and the other artificial. The health and happiness of future generations, indeed the health and happiness of all species, could well depend upon which of these paths we choose.

Fortunately, our efforts paid off. With the help of local organic growers, the California Rice Association, and surprisingly, a multibillion-dollar beer company that uses rice in its product, GM rice was rejected in California.

Edward Esko

We were, for the time being at least, able to preserve the organic crop in the Sacramento Valley. The implications extend far beyond growers and consumers. A variety of species depend upon the organic rice fields for habitat. According to farmwater.org:

> Rice has become one of the primary crops planted in the Sacramento Valley with farmers regularly planting about 550,000 acres each year. During the growing season the rice fields provide habitat to multiple species, including the endangered giant garter snake. Following harvest, more than 1.5 million ducks and 750,000 geese traveling the Pacific Flyway will use the rice fields as a stopover point to rest and feed. –"Rice importance extends to wildlife," farmwater.org.

The next major development in my lifelong engagement with rice occurred about ten years later. It was then that I became aware that rice was being successfully grown in the Northeastern U.S., not far from my home in Massachusetts. Ever since my visit to Japan, I had dreamt of someday seeing rice fields and paddies across the length and breadth of the Eastern Seaboard, from Maine to Florida. Soon after returning from the Sacramento Valley, in the early 2000s, I planted rice seed from Lundberg Farms in my backyard garden. The seeds required regular watering. By early summer they had sprouted and grew normally. The flag leaf and heads began to form as the summer progressed. But when early fall arrived, it became apparent that the rice grains would not mature fully. The reason, I believe, was because the seeds were adapted to the relatively mild climate of Northern California, and not the rigorous mountain climate of the Berkshires.

Several years later, however, I got the news about the successful cultivation of rice in New England. Apparently, organic growers had obtained seed from a northern region of Japan, in addition to Duborskian seed from Russia. These more robust varieties had no problem with the cooler temperatures and shorter growing season in the Northeastern U.S. The main proponent of the Duborskian rice was Christian Elwell, founder of the South River Miso Company in Conway, Massachusetts. Christian is famous for producing high-quality handcrafted miso using time-tested methods and organic ingredients. I had known Christian for many years. He and I had worked together back in the 1970s, assisting Michio Kushi in Boston. Christian had been growing dryland rice for over 30 years at his farm, and was experimenting with growing it in a small circular paddy.

It was after many visits to South River and discussions with Christian that I began to appreciate the influence of the awns, the delicate hairlike projections extending from each grain, not only on the growth and development of the rice, but also on the body, mind, and spirit of those who eat rice as food. The Duborskian rice that Christian is growing is a long-awned variety, in contrast to commercial rice, which has had the awns bred out of the seed stock. (Awns are characteristic of the cereals as a whole. They are especially noticeable on grains such as barley, wheat, and rye.) The insights in this book relating to the awns are due largely to in-the-field discussions with Christian during various stages of the rice cycle. At the same time, I was pleased to discover that organic growers in Vermont, Maine, New York, and New Jersey were also successfully growing rice, some commercially. I have included their stories in the Appendix, *Growing Rice in New England*. These stories were first published by Amberwaves Press in the 2017 book, *The Rice Revolution*.

As you will discover in this book, the quality of rice and other foods we eat has a profound effect on our body, mind, and spirit. Basing our diet on lightfoods, those which directly channel and store energy from the sun and cosmos, in their whole natural form, maximizes our potential for health, consciousness, and spiritual development. A lightfood diet can facilitate not only personal health and development, but also the health and wellbeing of society as a whole. Lightfoods are the vehicle that make it possible for humanity to enter into a future of health, sustainability, and peace, in accord with the cycles of nature and the universe.

Edward Esko
Berkshire, Massachusetts

Notes from the Editor

I have known about macrobiotics for as long as I can remember. My grandmother began practicing macrobiotics following a grim diagnosis of cancer at the age of 66. I grew up watching her eat miso soup in the morning, and beans, grains, brown rice and vegetables for lunch and supper. My grandmother passed away just weeks before her 90th birthday, 24 years after being given only 6 months to live. I have endless memories of my grandmother and some of my most favorite memories were made in the heart of her home, the kitchen. In her kitchen I played card games over a cup of tea, engaged in meaningful conversations, learned to sew my first quilt, and tasted my first macrobiotic food.

When my grandmother began practicing macrobiotics, she switched from cooking with electricity to cooking with wood. Her wood powered range made its presence known, inserting itself towards the center of the room. My childhood memories are of a cast iron cooktop with removable hot plate burners that could be lifted with a lifting device, exposing the fire below and allowing more wood to be dropped into the flames. The popping and crackling sounds of the fire provided the perfect ambiance for the activities taking place at the nearby kitchen table. The range served to prepare food, and it also filled the room with a comfortable warmth during cold winter days. After playing in the snow while visiting at our grandmother's home, my cousins and I would hang our wet mittens behind the stove and place our boots to dry. Then we would perch ourselves at the front of the stove, hovering our hands over the cooktop to warm up. Then one day, that old cookstove had to be removed from the home because it no longer passed fire inspection codes. It was a sad time for me. It was like the heart of the kitchen had been removed. The wood range was replaced with a gas-range, not entirely the same, but it still gave Grammie the ability to cook with fire, and that was important.

A few years ago, with my grandmother as my inspiration, I began studying at the International Macrobiotic Institute, listening to the life-changing teachings of a world leader in macrobiotics and the author of this book, Edward Esko. With this book he continues to inspire, providing the reader with an innovative, yet time-honored, explanation about how eating a plant-based, whole-grain centered diet influences our physical and energetic body. He explores the dangers of a modern diet and its risk of disease for the human population, and its unsustainability for our planet, warning of a potential "collision between humanity and Earth." He brings to light Michio Kushi's *Spiral of History*, touching on pivotal milestones and providing hope for a peaceful future.

Whether you have been practicing macrobiotics for many years, or you are just beginning your journey, this book takes our understanding of food, and of food preparation, to a whole new level. Using the simple, yet insightful concept of the polarizing energies of yin and yang, we can see how plant food, in particular brown rice, can create harmony within the physical body, the energetic body, across our planet, and into the universe. I trust that when you finish reading this book you will be inspired to nourish your own body and spirit, with foods manifested from light, allowing you to be your own pioneer towards enlightenment.

Robin Brewer
April 5, 2021

Acknowledgements

I would like to thank all those who contributed to making this book possible. I thank the goddess Demeter (Ceres), who is credited with introducing cereal grains to humanity in the ancient past, as well as her fellow gods and goddesses who performed a similar task, and who are found in myths and legends the world over. I also thank the unknown ancestors who first applied fire, in the form of cooking, to the preparation of daily food, thus setting the stage for unlimited freedom and development. I thank the great philosophers, agriculturists, and healers, including the legendary Chinese Emperors—Fu Xi, Shennong (the Divine Farmer), and Huangdi (the Yellow Emperor), who observed the order of the universe and applied it to diet, agriculture, medicine, and all aspects of daily life.

I also thank those who in modern times, were part of my immediate circle. George Ohsawa, who I never met, I thank for interpreting the traditional philosophy and cosmology of the Far East and spreading it around the world under the name "macrobiotics." George's wife Lima Ohsawa, whom I did have the honor to meet and learn from, was an inspiration and guiding light, especially in her mastery of the art of organic brown rice-based cooking. Lima's birth name was *Sanae*, which means the "first sprouts of grain."

I especially thank my teacher, Michio Kushi, and his wife Aveline, who planted the seeds of many of the ideas that appear in this book. I also thank other macrobiotic predecessors, like Herman and Cornellia Aihara, William Dufty, and Shizuko Yamamoto, as well as my contemporary associates and fellow teachers, especially Bill Tara and Alex Jack. I thank my students and friends at the International Macrobiotic Institute (IMI.) They join our regular online studies from around the world, and will guide the world toward health and peace in the future. I also wish to thank the modern day divine farmers, the Lundberg family in California, Christian

Edward Esko

Elwell in Massachusetts, and our rice-growing friends in Vermont, Maine, New York, New Jersey and elsewhere in North America who are forging ahead with a model of agriculture based on genuine sustainability. I extend special thanks to Robin Brewer, an IMI graduate from New Brunswick, Canada, for her wonderful job editing and clarifying my writing. I thank my beloved parents, Ed Sr. and Liz, for their unwavering support over the years, as well as all the members of the ever-growing Esko clan. Finally, I would like to express my deepest gratitude to my wife, Naomi Ichikawa Esko, for her fabulous artwork and calligraphy, and for her love, support, and inspiration. –E.E.

The work on the circulation of the light depends entirely on the backward-flowing movement, so that the thoughts (the place of heavenly consciousness, the heavenly heart) are gathered together. The heavenly heart lies between the sun and moon (the two eyes.)
THE SECRET OF THE GOLDEN FLOWER (T'AI I CHIN HUA TSUNG CHIH)

Food systems have the potential to nurture human health and support environmental sustainability, however our current trajectories threaten both. The EAT–*Lancet* Commission addresses the need to feed a growing global population a healthy diet while also defining sustainable food systems that will minimize damage to our planet. The Commission quantitively describes a universal healthy reference diet, based on an increase in consumption of healthy foods (such as vegetables, fruits, whole grains, legumes, and nuts), and a decrease in consumption of unhealthy foods (such as red meat, sugar, and refined grains) that would provide major health benefits, and also increase the likelihood of attainment of the Sustainable Development Goals. This is set against the backdrop of defined scientific boundaries that would ensure a safe operating space within six Earth systems, towards sustaining a healthy planet.

FOOD IN THE ANTHROPOCENE: THE EAT-*LANCET* COMMISSION ON HEALTHY DIETS FROM SUSTAINABLE FOOD SYSTEMS

1

CRYSTALIZED LIGHT

As do other plants, cereal grains capture sunlight. During the day, cereal plants face the sun. The leaves capture sunlight and, through a process known as photosynthesis, combine it with carbon dioxide from the air and water from the soil. Light is captured and stored in the form of a simple carbohydrate known as glucose. In highly developed plants such as cereal grains, captured sunlight is used to form long-chained molecules known as complex carbohydrates.

When we eat a food such as rice or barley, we break these chains down into a single molecule—glucose—and release the stored light and energy. We burn the sun's energy at the cellular level. We use it to generate the heat and energy necessary for life. Our brain is especially dependent upon glucose, both for its baseline functions and to produce biophotons, which are biological particles of light. Biophotons originate with the sunlight captured by cereal grains and other plants. The brain, in turn, uses captured sunlight to generate the biophotons that facilitate day-to-day consciousness.

Cereal grains are unique. Along with sunlight, they capture a different, subtler type of energy. Cereal plants grow vertically and have antenna-like projections, known as awns, that extend up toward the sky. At night, the awns collect energy from the stars and other celestial bodies. The vibrations channeled by the awns are subtler than the visible light absorbed by the leaves. Nighttime energy has a shorter wavelength. It originates in the billions of stars, planets, galaxies, and other celestial bodies found in the universe at large. Much of this nighttime vibration exists outside the visible spectrum. It is too subtle to be detected by the physical senses.

Grains such as rice, barley, wheat, millet, and oats thus capture two types of energy, the energy of the sun during the day, and the subtle vibrations of the cosmos at night. All plants store sunlight through photosynthesis. However, only the cereal grains stand upright and channel, directly through their antennae-like awns, the full spectrum of nighttime energy. Sunlight animates daily consciousness and thinking. For example, our sense of sight is active during the day, as are the other forms of sensory awareness. On the other hand, our brain channels a subtler form of energy at night. These subtle vibrations originate from the distant universe. These are the same energies channeled through the awns of the cereal plant. At night, or during meditation, we close off the senses and quiet the mind. The production of biophotons diminishes during meditation or sleep. We can compare the opposite forms of energy channeled during the day and at night as follows:

Day	Night
Bright	Dark
Sun	Stars
Leaves	Awns
Horizontal	Vertical
Light capture	Vibration capture
Photosynthesis	Vibrational synthesis
Long wave	Short wave
Near space	Deep space
Solar	Galactic and beyond
Chemical	Energetic
Production of glucose	Storage of energy and information
Sensory	Ultra-sensory

The growth pattern of cereal grains offers a clue as to how the energies of day and night are captured by the plant. The natural world is governed by cycles, and these cycles are animated by the forces of heaven and Earth. In the spring, Earth's rising upward energy is dominant. Rice seeds are germinated indoors in small beds. The seeds put out roots while sprouts emerge and begin to shoot upward. Green, the color of the rice seedlings, is the color of spring. As the shoots grow, the rice paddy, which was dry over the winter, is flooded. When the shoots reach a height above the water level, they are taken outside and transplanted in evenly spaced rows. Transplantation was traditionally done by hand, and considered one of the most important events of the year. The rows in the paddy provide space for the plants to grow and produce the maximum number of seeds.

Like other cereals, rice will grow on dry land. The reason for the water-filled paddy is twofold. First, flooding eliminates weeds that could serve as competition for the rice. Second, the water absorbs heat during the day. It retains heat during cool spring nights. Like a blanket, it keeps the seedlings warm, allowing them to survive cool nighttime temperatures. This method of growing rice is truly sustainable. It has essentially continued unchanged for thousands of years. Ancient philosophers gave the upward energy of spring the iconic name, "Tree." The tree icon conjures an image of things growing up above the ground. The germinating and planting stages are perfect examples of this tree energy. Through the spring and into summer, the rice continues growing. Tadpoles appear in the paddy, while tiny green frogs appear on the rice plants. Their song enlivens the rice field. Under the influence of expansive force, the rice plant matures and reaches a height of 3 to 4 feet. It produces a reproductive stem known as a tiller. As expansive force reaches a peak, the stem will produce a flower head, often referred to as a spike. Each spike will then produce up to 150 tiny flowers. Once pollinated, the flowers form seeds.

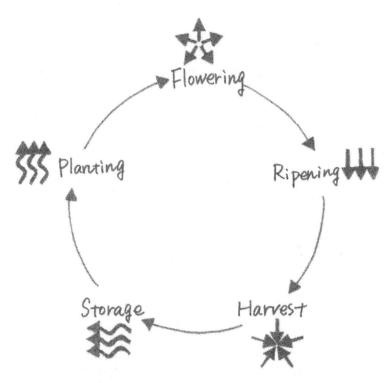

The five stages of the rice cycle. Illustration by Naomi Ichikawa Esko

Ancient philosophers gave the highly expansive energy of summer the iconic name "Fire." The fire icon generates an image of things reaching their peak of expansion. Flowers represent the peak of expansive energy. At this time, dragonflies appear and dart in and out of the rice paddy. Their distinctive buzz becomes part of the natural ecosystem. Seed formation is the beginning of the process in which the expansive energy of summer begins to move in the opposite direction. In comparison to flowers, seeds are dry and compact. Next comes the ripening stage in which the seeds turn golden. This occurs in late summer amidst an overall trend toward downward energy. Ancient philosophers gave the energy of late summer the iconic name "Soil." The soil icon conjures the image of soil or Earth, which are dense and compact in relation to tree or fire. As we enter autumn, the seeds become highly compact. Energy is being stored in each grain. The heads become heavier and bend down. Finally, at the peak of ripening, the rice is ready for harvest. At that time, the rice paddy is drained. The rice is hand cut with curved metal knives, stacked, bundled, and hung upside down to dry. Rice harvest is a very important time of year, equal to rice planting in traditional societies. Following harvest, people held festivals to celebrate the new crop and enjoy the abundance of nature. Ancient philosophers gave the highly condensed energy of autumn the iconic name "Metal." Metal has the most condensed energy in the cycle. At harvest, the rice undergoes a complete reversal in polarity. The grains, which point upward during the growing process, are now hung upside down, facing the Earth. Once the rice has dried, it is then threshed, or separated from the stalk.

The threshed grains are then collected and stored. The rice initially has its outer coat, or husk, attached. Some of this rice is put aside as seed for the next season. Some is hulled, meaning the inedible coat is removed. Freshly hulled brown rice has the strongest life energy of any variety of rice. The stage in which rice is stored, either for seed or in the pantry as food, corresponds to the dormant season of winter. Ancient philosophers gave that season the iconic name "Water." Water represents a phase in which atmospheric energy floats between heaven and Earth, or contraction and expansion. It is the time of rest and dormancy in preparation for the rising and awakening energy of the coming spring.

A crucial turning point in the rice cycle occurs in the middle of summer, during the plant's flowering stage. That is when the forces of heaven and Earth, sky and sun, night and day coalesce. Writing in *Macrobiotics Today* about the rice cycle at South River, author Mark Leonas describes this process:

> By August, all the plants are in the flowering stage. Each plant has a "flag leaf," which is the uppermost leaf below the "panicle" or cluster of loose branching flowers on the rice plant that will become the actual rice grains. The flag leaf and the other leaves are responsible for absorbing sunlight and photosynthetic energy, which direct the development of the plant. Etheric energy couples with photosynthetic energy to create a thickening stalk, the panicle, and the awns. The awns are conductors of even more energy absorption.

Christian Elwell, founder of South River Farm, marvels at the glistening upward reaching presence of the awns during the sunny August days. Under the ripening sun, the rice growth advances from vegetative stage to reproductive stage. Then the ripening begins and grains enter the milk stage, where they grow and fill out with a "skin" that is forming and hardening in the August sun. The etheric forces are now congealing grain milk in the hardening grains. The maturity of the grain is near, and it's an exciting time. As the summer sun wanes and crops come to full fruition, the rice plants now reach maturity with awns and rice leaves waving in the early fall breezes. The rice milk hardens into fully formed grains.

Awned rice under the summer sun

A miraculous process takes place under the summer sky. During the plant's flowering stage, the grain milk is a thick liquid that is sensitive to vibrations. The energy of the night sky travels down through the awn, where it leaves a subtle imprint, not unlike a footprint in wet sand. Water may hold the key to the transmission and storage of this information. According to researcher Masaru Emoto, author of *The Hidden Messages in Water,* "water has the ability to *copy* and *memorize* information." Emoto observed and photographed the structure of crystals formed in water exposed to positive thoughts, images, words, and beautiful harmonious music, and compared those to the crystals formed in water exposed to negative thoughts, images, words, and discordant, chaotic, and unpleasant sounds. He found that positive vibrations produced well-formed crystals of incredible elegance, symmetry, and beauty, while negative or discordant vibrations resulted in "fragmented and malformed crystals at best." Emoto stated, "And I have found the most beautiful crystal of all—the one created by 'love and gratitude.' This is supposedly what all the world's religions are founded on, and if that were true, there would be no need for laws. Love and gratitude are the words that must serve as the guide for the world."

The sum total of vibration channeled at night through the awns and captured by the water in each developing grain can be summarized in the words "love and gratitude." That vibrational pattern influences the patterning of the carbohydrate and protein molecules in each grain. It then solidifies into a crystalline structure as the grains harden in the summer sun. I asked rice farmer Christian Elwell about the timeframe in which this process takes place. Christian replied that the window was narrow; perhaps a ten-day period in July or August when the awns are viable and the rice milk soft and malleable. That window is of course variable. It depends on the type of grain, the latitude of the field, the amount of water available, weather, and other factors. Once the imprint has been received, the template is baked in the midday sun. Like cuneiform script etched into clay tablets and placed in an oven to harden, the vibrational imprint is hardwired into each grain. The grains are like biologically active microchips that store information received from the cosmos, in addition to concentrating the energy received from the sun.

Awned, or "long-awned" rice, such as that grown at South River, is rare in the modern world, although the original species contained fully developed awns. The species grown at South River, known as "Duborskian" rice, comes most recently from Ukraine and Russia, and before that, Italy and China. It is a dry land variety that also grows in a paddy and yields beautiful tall plants and long awns. It readily adapts to temperate climates such as those in North America. Other grains, such as wheat and barley, still retain long or developed awns. According to the paper, "Convergent Loss of Awn in Two Cultivated Rice Species Oryza sativa and Oryza glaberrima is Caused by Mutations in Different Loci" (ncbi.nlm.nih.gov):

> A long awn is one of the distinct morphological features of wild rice species. This organ is thought to aid in seed dispersal and prevent pre-dation by animals. Most cultivated varieties of *Oryza sativa* and *Oryza glaberrima*, however, have lost the ability to form long awns. The causal genetic factors responsible for the loss of awn in these two rice species remain largely unknown.

The authors go on to state:

> The awn, a typical feature of Poaceae, is a needle-like organ extending from the tip of the lemma and is considered to be a modified leaf blade. This bristly, barbed extension of the spikelet facilitates seed dispersal by attaching the seed to animal fur and deters seed predation by birds and mammals. In some cases, such as in wild tetraploid wheat, the movement of awns may even propel the seed into soil. Despite the important roles of grass awns under wild conditions, long and barbed awns hinder manual harvesting under agricultural conditions and have largely been avoided during artificial selection of rice by humans. In contrast to barley awns, which are capable of photosynthesis during grain-filling, rice awns lack chlorenchyma and cannot contribute to photosynthesis. Consistent with that observation, removal of awns has been shown to have a negligible effect on rice grain maturation and,

consequently, cultivated rice varieties may have become awnless to enhance ease of harvest without adverse effects on yield.

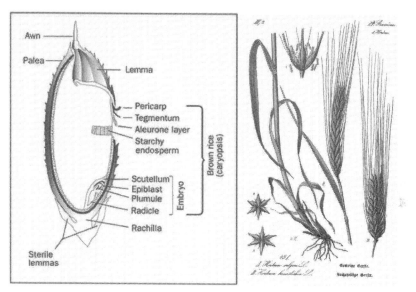

Cross section of unhulled brown rice (left) shows an abbreviated awn at the top.
Barley, at right, offers a clear example of a long-awned cereal crop

Even though long awns are rare in modern rice, an awn stub or bud is nevertheless present in short-awned varieties. The abbreviated awn is able to serve as a conduit for cosmic energy, although not to the degree of a long awn. The longer the awn, the deeper into the universe the message of love and gratitude originates, with greater depth and power.

2

EARTHLY ROOTS

Daytime energy originates with the sun: nighttime energy with stars and celestial bodies. Both originate above and beyond the planet, and spiral in toward the Earth. We can visualize the sum of these forces as two hands molding a snowball. The hands exert roughly equal pressure in all directions. This is true not only for the Earth, but also for the sun, stars, planets, moons, and other celestial bodies, so that during their formative stages, all of these celestial bodies take the form of a sphere. Ancient people referred to the imaginary hands as "heaven's" force. In the I Ching, the foundational book of oriental cosmology, this power is referred to as Ch'ien, or the Creative, and is symbolized in the form of an icon, known as a hexagram, consisting of six unbroken parallel lines.

> These unbroken lines stand for the primal power, which is light-giving, active, strong, and of the spirit. The hexagram [icon] is consistently strong in character, and since it is without weakness, its essence is power or energy. Its image is heaven. Its energy is represented as unrestricted by any fixed conditions in space and is therefore conceived of as motion. Time is regarded as the basis of this motion. Thus, the hexagram includes also the power of time and the power of persisting in time, that is, duration. –The I Ching, or Book of Changes, Wilhelm/Baynes

Meanwhile, the Earth generates a completely opposite type of energy. The invisible hands can't keep pressing inward. The planet's solid mass generates resistance, something like a "bounce." Not only does the incoming force produce its opposite, in the form of resistance, it also produces movement, in the form of rotation. Thus, the Earth is a gigantic spinning gyroscope. Nonstop rotation produces powerful upward or centrifugal forces that spiral outward. This energy appears across the planet in the form of upward motion. The force of the planet was given the name "Earth's" force. The I Ching refers to it as K'u, or the Receptive, and symbolizes it in the form of six divided or broken parallel lines. According to Wilhelm and Baynes:

> The attribute of the hexagram is devotion; its image is the earth. It is the perfect complement of the Creative—the complement, not the opposite, for the Receptive does not combat the Creative but completes it. It represents nature in contrast to spirit, earth in contrast to heaven, space as against time, the female-maternal as against the male paternal.

Everything on the planet, and the planet itself, is formed and animated by the two forces. The I Ching points out that all things on Earth and in heaven are changing. Change is animated by these two opposite energies and found everywhere in the universe, not only on Earth. Change occurs in cycles that alternate from one tendency to the other and back again. Earth's force drives the upward flow of water through the soil and atmosphere. Heaven's force causes condensation and the falling of rain and snow. Heaven and Earth drive the multiple cycles of the biosphere, including those of carbon, oxygen, and nitrogen, as well as the planet's climate, weather, geology, atmosphere, and the life cycle of plants and animals.

Heaven's force drives the movement of water from the atmosphere down into the soil. Earth's force causes water to be absorbed by the roots and move upward through the plant. Heaven's force drives nitrogen (N_2) from the atmosphere down to the Earth where bacteria in the soil fix or concentrate it in the form of compounds like nitrite and ammonia, which are the precursors of amino acids and proteins. Earth's force liberates nitrogen from decaying biological matter and releases it back into the atmosphere. Plants absorb carbon dioxide and water and combine it with sunlight to form carbohydrate in the process of photosynthesis. This process occurs due to the influence of heaven's force. Earth's force facilitates the release of these substances in the animal body through the process of respiration, or burning. In the biological world, the interplay of heaven and Earth produces two complementary yet antagonistic macronutrients, carbohydrate and protein. Carbon-based carbohydrates are the product of the sun and atmosphere; while nitrogen-based protein is the product of the Earth.

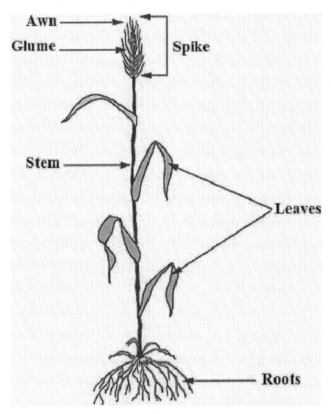

In the cereal plant, leaves capture energy from the sun, forming carbohydrate.
Energy from the Earth flows up through the roots and is used to form protein.
The awns at the top channel energy from the universe as a whole

Living in the soil are bacteria that are able to fix or capture nitrogen from the air. (Nitrogen makes up about 78% of the atmosphere; while oxygen comprises about 21%.) Bacteria convert this nitrogen into nitrite, which, together with water, is absorbed by the roots of the plant. These products of the Earth flow up from the ground. Nitrite from the soil combines with glucose, or sun-sourced carbohydrate, to form amino acids. Carbohydrate is thus the base material in the formation of the amino acids, and eventually the protein, produced by the plant. Carbohydrates are the direct product of the sun, while proteins are cycled through the soil and are the product of the Earth. Thus, carbohydrates are used for energy, like that of the sun, and proteins are used to build physical structure, originating in the Earth.

Rice is unique in that it is able to grow in water. It takes advantage of soil-based bacteria as well as species of blue-green algae to fix nitrogen. The historical development of this hybrid process in China is described in the publication, *The Nitrogen Fixation and Its Research in China*, pp 323-437:

The rice paddy fields in China are mainly distributed in the southern provinces in the subtropical and temperate climatic regions. The Yangtze River Valley is the center of rice plantation, which stretches from the east coast to the western mountainous areas of Szechuan and Yunnan provinces. This vast area of more than 20 million hectares of rice paddy fields have gone through several hundreds of years of agricultural practices of rice-green manure and rice-wheat or rape types of paddy/dryland rotational farming. A type of humus-rich and high N-content rice paddy soil has been developed with high productivity for grains (Xiong and Li 1987). Farmers used to grow a crop of leguminous green manure, milk vetch (*Astragalus*) or vetch (*Vicia*) after rice harvesting in late autumn for the effect of symbiotic nitrogen fixation of *Rhizobium* and to use it as base manure to supply organic matter and nitrogen for the next rice crop (Chiao 1986). During the growing period of rice plants, in addition to the different naturally developed filamentous and unicellular nitrogen-fixing blue-green algae in the stagnant water layer of the rice field, farmers also grow *Azolla* in the rice fields serving as top-dressing green manure to supply nitrogen and other nutrients (Liu 1981). *Azolla* infected with a blue-green alga, *Anabaena azollae*, is a very effective symbiotic nitrogen fixation system on shallow water surface in temperature regions. Thus the opportunities of free-living and symbiotic blue-green algae for nitrogen fixation come into full play in Chinese rice paddy fields.

Cereal grains are a form of grass. The grasses appeared around 55 million years ago. There are more than 12,000 species distributed across every continent. Grasses are the primary source of the worlds's dietary energy. Through direct human consumption, grasses provide 51% of all nutritional energy; rice provides 20%, wheat makes up 20%, corn (maize) 5.5%, and other grains 6%. Among the grasses, cereals are unique in that they exhibit a consistent ratio in their nutrient composition. This is apparent in their ratio of carbohydrate to protein. Millet, for example, contains on average 70 grams of carbohydrate and 10 grams of protein, in a ratio of seven to one. Rice is near this proportion, with approximately 77 grams of carbohydrate to 10 grams of protein and fat. (Quantities are per 100 grams. Source: U.S. Dept. of Agriculture.) These figures of course depend on the sample being analyzed. There is variation between varieties, for example, between short, long, and medium rice, and between crops grown with chemicals and those grown organically.

Not surprisingly, human teeth display a similar pattern, with a seven to one ratio between carbohydrate (plant) processing teeth to protein (animal) processing teeth. The majority of the teeth (28 molars, premolars, and incisors) are crushing, grinding, and cutting teeth, indicating that throughout our history, plant foods—which are predominately carbohydrate—comprised the bulk of the human diet. The four canine teeth suggest that animal food—which is predominately protein—played a less important role in evolutionary development. The pattern of the teeth casts doubt on the Man-the-Hunter hypothesis, popular among anthropologists, which states that our ancestors evolved toward homo sapiens as the result of hunting and meat-eating. New evidence is calling into question that assumption.

Often referred to as the expensive tissue hypothesis, the widely accepted claim that our brain size and complexity are connected to eating animals has been rigorously tested and refuted in a key report published in *Nature* (Navarrete, 2011). This comprehensive report evaluates the research into more than 100 mammalian species, including 23 primate species, analyzing brain size and organ mass data. Lead researcher Navarrete concludes that, "human encephalization (brain development) was made possible by a combination of stabilization of energy inputs and a redirection of energy from locomotion, growth and reproduction." Then in 2015 a study published in *The Quarterly Review of Biology*, led by Dr. Karen Hardy, compiles archaeological, anthropological, genetic, physiological and anatomical evidence to argue that carbohydrate consumption, particularly in the form of starch, was critical for the accelerated expansion of the human brain over the last million years. –Robert Grillo, "Examining the Claim, Our Brains Evolved from Eating Animals," freefromharm.org.

The seven to one ratio appears at the opposite end of the digestive tract, in the colon. An astonishing 100 trillion bacteria inhabit the large intestine in a vast ecosystem known as the *microbiome*. Here the ratio of "good" bacteria to "bad" bacteria is 85% to 15%, or seven to one. So-called "good" bacteria, such as lactobacillus and lactobacillus bifidus, are strengthened and augmented by the intake of prebiotics and probiotics. Prebiotics are undigested plant fibers and resistant starches. They serve as food for beneficial bacteria in the digestive tract. Probiotics are the living microorganisms found in fermented foods like miso, natto, and sauerkraut. These foods directly augment and strengthen the "good" bacteria in the colon. On the other hand, animal proteins decompose into a variety of harmful substances, including gram-negative bacteria, toxic metabolites, and ammonia.

A high-meat diet overwhelms the body's ability to digest protein, so that as much as 12 grams of protein go undigested and unabsorbed, and enter the colon. Here the protein begins to decompose and produce harmful bacteria and other toxic substances. These bad actors are responsible for a variety of pathological and potentially life-threatening conditions. Like the teeth, the structure and composition of the colon suggests an evolutionary advantage to a diet based on whole grains and other plant foods.

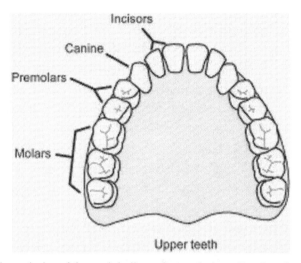

The majority of the teeth indicate that evolutionarily, plant foods
comprised the bulk of the human diet. The four canine teeth
suggest that animal foods played a less important role

Not only do the teeth suggest that a plant-based diet was central to human development, but they also offer further clues as to the composition of the ideal diet moving forward. Of the plant processing teeth, the majority (20) are molars and premolars suited for crushing and grinding whole grains, beans, seeds, and other tough plant fibers. The minority (8) are the front incisors, which are well suited for cutting vegetables. Here we see that the ratio of hard fibers, like those in whole grains, beans, and seeds, to the softer fibers in vegetables, is 20 to 8, or a little more than 2 to 1.

Maintaining a 2 to 1 ratio between hard and soft fibers conveys a number of advantages. The emphasis on the ample protein in whole grains, beans, and seeds helps ensure that one's diet provides an adequate supply of both carbohydrate and protein. A diet based on raw fruits and vegetables cannot make this claim. Diets that de-emphasize the intake of whole grains and beans in favor of fruits and vegetables tend to be deficient in protein, as well as in complex carbohydrate, the other essential macronutrient. Furthermore, emphasizing grains and beans necessitates cooking. These plant fibers are hard in their raw state and require softening to make them edible. Cooking (as well as soaking, sprouting, and fermenting) softens the plant fibers and facilitates smooth digestion, thorough absorption, and the efficient release of energy. Cooking is a form of pre-digestion that makes additional energy available to the body. It is also part of our heritage. Humans have been cooking for at least 2 million years.

In the realm of whole grains, there are two principal categories: the first is brown rice and the second is whole wheat. They are the alpha and omega of the world's cereal crops. Rice is the primary grain of Asia, while wheat is a staple food in the Middle East, India, Europe, and America. The difference between these two staple grains is vast; it determines the very nature of the cultures and civilizations that eat them. Brown rice can be eaten as is and is sweet, chewy, and satisfying. It only needs to be boiled or pressure cooked and served along with soup, vegetable, bean, and other side dishes. By eating whole unrefined rice as your main food, you are receiving its nutrients in their intact and balanced form. Whole wheat is a different story. Many years ago, I bought a pound of organic wheat berries and boiled them as you would brown rice. That was to be my grain of the day. As I quickly discovered, whole wheat kernels are very chewy. They have a somewhat tangy, and not a particularly sweet taste. Wheat is higher in protein than rice, with about twice as much protein.

Many thousands of years ago, our ancestors probably got tired of chewing the tough wheat grains. Being inventive, they developed techniques for crushing or milling grains into flour. Milling, or grinding the grain between stones, is a form of external chewing. Our crushing or grinding teeth are known as "molars." (The word "molar" is Latin for "millstone.") Milling opened the door to a range of enjoyable foods, such as sourdough bread, flatbread, chapati, noodles, and pasta, which in comparison to wheat kernels, are fun (i.e., noodles), delicious, and user-friendly. Milling wheat into flour made the tough wheat grains (and the protein they contain) easily accessible. However, what happens when whole grains are crushed into flour? Whole grains are intact seeds and thus contain vital life force. That life force disappears when grains are crushed. Also, over time flour begins to lose nutrients through oxidation. As a result, additional side dishes, in some cases including animal food, are required to make up for the missing nutrients. Western culture is characterized by wheat flour and animal food.

On the other hand, with whole brown rice as the main grain, however, it is easier to get by with fewer side dishes and animal products.

The rise in gluten sensitivity is due largely to the development of high-yield hybridized wheat and other grains. Hybridized wheat is known as "dwarf" wheat. Heirloom wheat, which humanity has eaten for at least 10,000 years, is a delicate grass. Its gluten, or protein, is easy for the digestive system to break down. With the exception of those with celiac disease, a genetically predisposed autoimmune disorder of the small intestine, heirloom wheat normally poses no problem for digestion or absorption when eaten in moderation. Compared to the delicate nature of heirloom wheat, modern hybridized dwarf varieties are tough, fibrous, and hard to digest. They are bred to readily absorb fertilizer. Until the last century, the human digestive tract had no experience in processing them. Writing in *The News Herald*, Theresa Edmunds describes the problem with modern hybridized wheat:

> Wheat has been hybridized during the last 50 years to such an extent that it has increased the gluten content exponentially. Not only that, hybridization has created new strains of gluten—one study found 14 new ones. Why was wheat hybridized? Originally it was to increase production and create hardy, pest-resistant wheat with a long shelf life. The man credited with breeding the high-yield dwarf wheat that is grown today is Norman Borlaug, who won the Nobel Peace Prize in 1970 for his work. Through this hybridization process, the gluten content increased but no testing was ever performed on animals or humans. The problem with gluten is that it is hard to digest and with wheat now containing so much of it, it is becoming a problem for many people.

There are several ways to reduce or avoid the problem of gluten sensitivity. First, avoid modern wheat products; second, base your diet on brown rice, millet, and other gluten-free whole grains and grain products; and third, shift to heirloom organic wheat, barely, and rye and the natural products made from these staples as soon as your digestion becomes strong enough. Each grain, including those containing gluten, has a unique beneficial effect on body and mind.

The nitrogen in animal protein increases the growth of bacteria. Eating less animal food, thus less protein, reduces the growth of bacteria, including the harmful bacteria that accompany the decomposition of animal flesh. On the other hand, carbon, such as that in carbohydrate, limits bacterial overgrowth. Studies show that plant eaters have the highest levels of carbon and lowest levels of nitrogen in the colon. Meat eaters have higher levels of nitrogen and lower levels of carbon. According to Katrine Whiteson, a microbiome researcher at the University of California, "Generally eating lots of plants and getting a lot of fiber is likely to be a healthy diet, and that by nature would mean eating less nitrogen." Microcosm equals macrocosm. What we do on a daily basis has a profound effect not only on our own health, but also on the health of the environment. This is especially true when it comes to what we eat. A 2017 article published on the website of the Weather Channel entitled, "Meat Industry to Blame for Largest-Ever 'Dead Zone' in Gulf of Mexico" describes one of the problems arising from the modern dependence upon animal proteins:

According to a report by the environmental group Mighty Earth, runoff from farms loaded with phosphorous and other toxins that come from manure and fertilizer has created toxic algae blooms that lead to oxygen-deprived dead zones that are becoming all too common from the Great Lakes to Chesapeake Bay. This week, the National Oceanic and Atmospheric Administration said this year's Gulf of Mexico dead zone is the biggest ever measured and covers an area the size of New Jersey. The Gulf dead zone forms each year when nitrogen-rich pollution flows from fields (mostly soy and corn fields used to feed livestock) into streams and rivers and ultimately into the Mississippi River. When the pollutants reach the Gulf, they form toxic algae blooms that decompose and choke off oxygen to marine life.

"Most of the nitrogen and phosphorous that drives this problem comes from the upper Midwest," former NOAA scientist and professor of environment and sustainability at the University of Michigan Don Scaia told NPR. "It's coming from agriculture." Last year, the United States Geological Survey said approximately 1.15 million metric tons of nitrogen pollution originating from farms flowed into the Gulf of Mexico. "As demand for meat grows, America's last native grassland prairies are being destroyed to make room for new industrial fields that exacerbate water pollution across the Heartland and take a heavy toll on the climate," said the release. In 2015, the U.S. produced 24 billion pounds of beef, 40 billion pounds of chicken and 25 billion pounds of pork.

Our diet, and in fact our existence itself, is the product of the ubiquitous forces of heaven and Earth, night and day, and darkness and light. Carbohydrates, which are the product of sunlight, in combination with water and carbon dioxide, represent the crystallization of heaven's energy. Protein, the product of nitrates in the soil, is primarily the product of the Earth. Carbohydrates originate in light; protein in darkness. The former is converted into energy, the latter used to form our physical body. The key issue in nutrition is the quality of each, and also the balance between the two. Cereal grains offer a template of balance between heaven and Earth, light and darkness, energy and physical form. Thus, cereal grains are the perfect centerpiece in the human diet.

Because raw eggs are technically chicken embryos, the effects of consuming raw eggs can be akin to the effects of consumption-based stem cell and placenta supplements.
GOOGLE

3

SENTIENCE

More than twenty years ago, the European Union attached a legally binding protocol to the Treaty of Amsterdam that recognized animals as sentient beings and required member states to pay full regard to the welfare requirements of animals. In 2012, a group of international scientists issued "The Cambridge Declaration on Consciousness" reaffirming animal sentience (see Appendix.) Sentience is defined as the capacity to feel, perceive, or experience subjectively. That animals possess sentience is not in question. The relevant question therefore is, "What are the effects of eating other sentient beings?" If animals feel pain and experience emotions, what, if any, effects do these have on the people who depend on them for food? Further, if animals possess sentience, what about plants? Does the effect of eating plants differ from the effect of eating animals? If so, how?

Diet has consequences, both positive and negative. There are a number of effects that arise from eating sentient creatures. Most apparent are the biochemical effects arising from the influence that hormones have on the muscles, cells, and tissues in the animal body. The stress experienced by an animal influences the quality of meat it produces. This is a major concern in the livestock industry. An article in the trade journal, *Food Technology,* titled, "Animal Welfare: Good for Livestock, Good for Business," with the subheading, "Poor Treatment = Poor Quality," addressed this issue. Similar findings appeared in the report, "Guidelines for Humane Handling, Transport and Slaughter of

Livestock," published by the Food and Agriculture Organization of the United Nations:

> Scientific research has shown that warm-blooded animals (this includes livestock) feel pain and the emotion of fear. In particular mammals, including food animals of this group, have brain structures that enable them to feel fear and suffering from pain, and it is likely that they suffer pain in the same way as humans. Fear and pain are very strong causes of stress in livestock and stress affects the quality of meat obtained from this livestock. Pain is usually the effect of injury and suffering, which also affects the quality and value of meat from affected animals.

Mammalian bodies need energy from the sun—in the form of glucose—for movement and life activity. This energy is stored in muscles in the form of glycogen. Healthy and well-rested animals have a high glycogen content in their muscles. When the animal is slaughtered, this glycogen is converted into lactic acid. This compound keeps the meat tender and flavorful. Fear and stress cause adrenaline to be released, and this depletes glycogen in the muscles and leads to changes in the meat. Meat from stressed animals is tough, dry, acidic, and dark in color. It goes bad quickly. In pigs the result of pre-slaughter stress is meat that is pale, acidic, and crumbly. It is known as PSE (pale, soft, exudative) meat. PSE cannot be sold, and the pork industry loses $275 million each year in discarded meat. The period just before slaughter is thought to be pivotal in determining how the meat turns out. Because animals are sentient, the fear and stress induced by slaughter produces quantifiable biochemical effects.

The second effect is less easily measurable. It is due to the influence of the brain and nervous system in producing what is known as cellular memory. Neuroscientists have discovered independent networks of neurons existing outside the brain, for example, in the heart and small intestine. Neuronal networks also exist throughout the body, including in the organs, muscles, and glands. One theory proposes that memory is stored in the synapses, or the spaces where signals pass between the nerve cells:

Once a memory is lost, is it gone forever? Most research points to yes. Yet a study published in the online journal *eLife* now suggests that traces of a lost memory might remain in a cell's nucleus, perhaps enabling future recall or at least the easy formation of a new, related memory. The current theory accepted by neurobiologists is that long-term memories live at synapses, which are the spaces where impulses pass from one nerve cell to another. Lasting memories are dependent on a strong network of such neural connections; memories weaken or fade if the synapses degrade. –"Could Memory Traces Exist in Cell Bodies?" *Scientific American,* May 1, 2015

These discoveries indicate that the tissues of the body perform not only physical functions, but also serve as repositories of consciousness and emotion. Consciousness and emotion leave a biochemical imprint. Evidence for that has been accumulating, especially among human organ transplant recipients. These discoveries could have profound implications for our understanding of the effects, both visible and invisible, not only of organ transplants, but also of eating the flesh of sentient animals.

One of the better-known instances of cellular memory is that of Claire Sylvia. Claire suffered from a rare degenerative lung disease and, to save her life, underwent a heart-and-lung transplant. She received the heart and lungs of an eighteen-year-old man who had died in a motorcycle accident. According to the notes in her fascinating book, *A Change of Heart* (Little, Brown and Company, 1997):

Even as she lay recovering in Intensive Care, Claire began to feel the presence of something or someone else within her. At first terrified and then fascinated, she soon noticed that her attitudes, habits, and tastes had changed. She had inexplicable cravings for food she had previously disliked. She found herself drawn to cool colors and no longer dressed in the vibrant reds and oranges she used to love. And she started behaving with an aggressiveness and impetuosity she had previously never shown. Five months after the operation she had a remarkable dream in which she met a young man named Tim L., a man she absolutely knew was her donor.

A subsequent meeting with her donor's family confirmed what she knew already: Tim L. was in fact the man who had donated his heart and lungs to her. In another well-known case, an eight-year-old girl received the heart of another young girl. Following the operation, she began to have a recurring nightmare in which she saw a man murdering a young girl. Her dreams were so realistic and disturbing that her parents took her to a psychiatrist who determined that her dreams were real. She was able to describe the scene in vivid detail, including the face of the attacker. When she went to the police, it was discovered that the young donor had in fact been murdered, and her description of the attacker was used to apprehend and convict the killer.

Although a number of theories have been put forward, such as the synapse theory mentioned above, science is for the most part at a loss to explain these occurrences. One theory states that neuropeptides, small protein-like molecules used by nerve cells to communicate with each other, may be storehouses for memory. Neuropeptides have recently been discovered to exist not only in the brain, but also throughout the body. Another theory, known as epigenetics, proposes that stress in the environment can affect the way in which the DNA of cells is expressed, without affecting the genetic code itself. Tiny chemical tags are added to or deleted from DNA in response to environmental influences, and these tags turn genes on or off, thus facilitating better adaptation to the environment. Studies support the idea that trauma leaves a lasting imprint that can be passed from generation to generation. It is thought that trauma affects RNA, the molecule that regulates the expression of genes.

Still another avenue of research is looking at the role that stem cells play in cellular memory. Stem cells are found in most of the body's tissues. They replenish cells as they age or die. They have the ability to differentiate into any one of the cell types that comprise human tissue. Stem cells also may be able to process and store memory. According to *Evolution News*:

Stem cells, famous for replenishing the body's stockpile of other cell types throughout life, may have an additional, unforeseen ability to cache memories of past wounds and inflammation. New studies in the skin, gut and airways suggest that stem cells, often in partnership with the immune system, can use these memories to improve the responses of tissues to later injuries and pathogenic assaults.

"What we are starting to realize is that these cells aren't just there to make tissue. They actually have other behavioral roles," said Shruti Naik, an immunologist at New York University who has studied this memory effect in skin and other tissues. Stem cells, she said, "have an exquisite ability to sense their environment and respond." –"Memory: New Research Reveals Cells Have It, Too," *Evolution News,* November 18, 2018

Humans and animals share basic biological functions. Animals possess cellular memory. The nonstop trauma, brutality, and degradation experienced by livestock animals leaves an indelible imprint on their cells and tissues, including cells in the milk they produce for their young. Admittedly, the instances of cellular memory being documented involve the living tissues of transplanted organs, whereas the muscles, tissues, and cells of cattle, pigs, sheep, and chickens being consumed are no longer alive. However, the repeated trauma experienced by the animal prior to slaughter most likely leaves a durable imprint (cellular memory) in its protein molecules, similar to the physical degradation noted in the meat of stressed animals, that remains long after the animal has been killed.

As it does with the storage of cosmic information in the cereal grains, water may play an important role in mediating the capture and storage of information in the protein molecules in animal food. As Masaru Emoto demonstrated, water is highly sensitive to the environment, including to the vibrations of light, sound, thought, and emotion. The nightmarish conditions in which most livestock animals live out their lives and meet their untimely deaths naturally produces a chaotic configuration in the water molecules in their bodies, like the chaotic and malformed crystals in Emoto's photographs. Water has a direct influence on the structure of protein molecules. According to the article, "Water Determines the Structure and Dynamics of Proteins," published in *Chemical Reviews*, May 17, 2016:

Water is an essential participant in the stability, structure, dynamics, and function of proteins and other biomolecules. Thermodynamically, changes in the aqueous environment affect the stability of biomolecules. Structurally, water participates chemically in the catalytic function of proteins and nucleic acids and physically in the collapse of the protein chain during folding through hydrophobic collapse and mediates binding through the hydrogen bond in complex formation. The recent advances in computer simulations and the enhanced sensitivity of experimental tools promise major advances in the understanding of protein dynamics, and water will surely be a protagonist.

Animal foods are mostly water and the quality of this water has a profound effect on their protein makeup. Beef, composed of muscle meat, is 65-75% water and 20% protein, as is chicken meat. Whole eggs are 74% water and 13% protein, while milk is 87% water and 13% solids. Water may turn out to be the medium for the conduction and capture of cellular memory frozen in the protein molecules of the dead animal.

Milk and eggs differ from meat in that they are the products of living beings. It is well known that breastfeeding protects babies from disease, and that a mother's cells are in her milk. Moreover, immune cells are transferred from mother to baby and this is recognized as a primary factor in protecting newborns from infections and other challenges. One type of immune cell, innate lymphoid cells, or ILCs, sets up temporary residence in the baby's digestive tract. These cells protect the newborn from infection and intestinal inflammation. These cells display cellular memory: they train the newborn's developing immune system and oversee establishment of the intestinal microbiome. ILCs signal the mother to change the composition of her milk to aid in fighting infection. In other words, breast milk changes in response to the needs of the infant.

These processes are not unique to humans but occur across the spectrum of mammal species. Clearly, milk is a vehicle for cellular and genetic memory. Could the treatment of animals in the modern dairy industry produce traumatic cellular memories that are transferred to their milk? Is it possible that these memories are transferred to those who consume their milk, or consume products made from their milk? The real life situation of cows in the dairy industry may help us answer these questions.

In reality, the daily practices of most dairy farms are more distressing than those of meat production. A mother cow only produces milk when she gets pregnant. So, starting from the age of 15 months, she will usually be artificially inseminated. Farmers mechanically draw semen from a bull, and then force the female cow into a narrow trap, known as a "cattle crush," where they will brutally impregnate her.

When she gives birth, her calf will typically be removed within 36 hours, so the farmers can steal and sell you the milk that is meant for her baby. Wildlife experts say that a strong bond between cow and calf is formed quickly after birth. Following that callous separation, the mother will bellow and scream for days, wondering where her baby is. The answer depends on the gender of the calf. If male, he will probably either be shot and tossed into a bin, or sold to be raised for veal, which delays his death by just a matter of months. But if the calf is female, she will usually be prepared for her own entry into dairy production, where she will face the same cycle of hell that her mother is trapped in: forced impregnation, the theft of her baby, and a return to the cattle crush two or three months later.

For at least six months of the year, she will often be confined inside dark sheds. But a growing number of dairy farms in Britain use a "zero-grazing system" in which cows spend their entire lives indoors, in increasingly intensive structures. Although growth hormones are banned in the UK and antibiotic use is limited, a dairy cow can be given reproductive hormones and prescribed antibiotics by a vet to ensure she is kept in a condition to produce an unnatural amount of milk. Under normal circumstances, she would generally only have a maximum of two liters of milk in her udder at any one time, but rapacious farmers may force her to carry 20 liters or more. Her udder becomes so heavy that it makes her lame and she often develops an agonizing infection called mastitis. The strain this puts on her body means she is exhausted by the age of five. Soon, her milk yield will no longer be considered profitable. Or she might simply collapse under the agony of it all. Either way, she will be dragged off by a tractor, squeezed into a cramped truck, and driven to the slaughterhouse, to be killed and turned into burgers or baby food. Her throat slit after five sad and torturous years—under natural circumstances she could live to 25. –Chas Newkey Burden, "Dairy is scary. The public are waking up to the darkest part of farming," *The Guardian,* March 30, 2017

If cellular memory is stored in protein, including the protein in milk known as casein, these memories apparently survive the process of pasteurization. Pasteurized and ultra-high temperature milks maintain protein and lactose content similar to raw milk, although their vitamins and bacteria are largely destroyed. The ongoing misery and sadness of the modern milk cow may thus be transferred to her milk, and offered up to consumers in a variety of appealing forms, such as ice cream, cheese, and frozen yogurt, all of which attempt to hide that grim reality.

Eggs may be repositories for an even greater degree of cellular memory. Eggs are essentially stem cells that have the ability to differentiate into the diverse cells and functions of a living organism. As we saw above, stem cells are recognized as carriers of cellular memory. Let us therefore ask, what types of cellular memory do modern laying hens transfer to their eggs? According to People for the Ethical Treatment of Animals (PETA):

The more than 300 million chickens used each year for their eggs endure a nightmare that lasts for two years Hens in egg factories have a large portion of their beaks cut off with a burning-hot blade within hours or days of birth. No painkillers are used. Birds are in pain both during and after the procedure. Chicks, who often have a hard time eating and drinking after their beaks are mutilated, can suffer from hunger and dehydration because their food and water intake is greatly reduced for several weeks after the procedure.

Hens are then shoved into tiny wire "battery" cages, which measure roughly 18 inches by 24 inches and hold up to 10 hens, each of whom has a wingspan up to 36 inches. Even in the best-case scenario, a hen spends her life crowded in a space about the size of a file drawer with several other hens, unable to lift a single wing.

The birds are crammed so closely together that although normally clean animals, they are forced to urinate and defecate on one another.

The stench of ammonia and feces hangs heavy in the air, and disease runs rampant in the filthy, cramped sheds. Many birds die, and survivors are often forced to live with their dead and dying cagemates, who are sometimes left to rot. The light in the sheds is constantly manipulated to maximize egg production. For two weeks at a time, the hens are fed only reduced-calorie feed. This process induces an extra laying cycle.

Male chicks are worthless to the egg industry, so every year, millions of them are suffocated or thrown into high-speed grinders, called "macerators," while they are still alive. After about two years in these conditions, the hens' bodies are exhausted, and their egg production drops. These "spent" hens are shipped to slaughterhouses, where their fragile legs are forced into shackles and their throats are cut. By the time they are sent to slaughter, roughly 30 percent of them are suffering from broken bones resulting from neglect, osteoporosis, and rough treatment. Their emaciated bodies are so damaged that their flesh can generally be used only for companion-animal food, but some of this meat has been used in the National School Lunch Program.

Some may argue that plants have sentience. Yes, plants, and especially seeds and grains, are concentrated centers of energy. They possess meridian channels. They are highly sensitive to changes in their environment. But these responses occur reflexively, without the self-awareness possessed by animals. As we saw in the example of rice and other cereals, plants are highly sensitive channels that absorb and store information from the Earth and sky. If plants possess any form of consciousness, that consciousness originates outside the plant. Plants are the direct channels of nature and the universe. Unlike animals with a developed nervous system, plants do not possess a sense of self that is separate from their surroundings. Plants *are* the surroundings. Nature and the environment are inputted and interpreted by the brain and nervous system of an animal. Thus, when we eat animals, we are not channeling the environment directly. We are instead processing the environment secondhand, after it has been independently channeled, assimilated, absorbed, and interpreted by the animal. Plants have no such interpretive function. Plants are channels, and in the case of seeds, storehouses for the intelligence of the universe. Eating them puts us in touch with that larger consciousness, without the interference or interpretation of another species. Plants are clear channels. Their energies are pure. They come to us directly from the universe without being processed by the brain, nervous system, and cellular memory of another sentient being.

Another thing to consider is that grains, beans, and vegetables are harvested at the end of their life cycle. Animals, on the other hand, are unnaturally killed before their natural lifespan has been completed. Some livestock farmers, in an attempt to appear environmentally friendly, use the term "harvest" to describe the slaughter of their animals. These animals are not allowed to complete their life cycle, but are killed prematurely. Don't be fooled by the language: slaughter is not harvest. Grains represent both the seed and fruit of the plant. They are produced in abundance. One grain of rice grows into a plant that yields about 1,000 new seeds. If each of these is planted in the following cycle, the yield is an astonishing *one million* new grains. Clearly the Earth provides an abundance of plant nourishment for our species, with more than enough to sustain humanity generation after generation.

In the early part of the sixth century a young man named Dositheus went on pilgrimage to Jerusalem. In one of the churches there he saw a fresco of the judgment of the soul, and was very drawn to it. As he stood, studying, a woman robed in purple (something prohibited to anyone but the Emperor or Empress) came up to him and began to speak to him about spiritual life. In conclusion she told him that if he sought salvation, he must never eat meat. She then vanished, and he realized that he had been speaking to the Virgin Mary. He followed her advice and is remembered as a saint on the nineteenth day of February every year.

ABBOT GEORGE BURKE

4

Spiritual Nutrition

Meditation and practices such as chanting, hymns, and choral music aim at increasing the frequency of the human vibratory field and expanding the scope of consciousness. They go hand in hand with a plant based diet. Conversely, spiritual traditions around the world teach that animal foods impede meditation and spiritual practices. Abbot George Burke, founder of the Light of the Spirit Monastery, states it thusly: "The effects of meat on the mental and psychic states of those who eat it is detrimental in the attempt at attaining higher consciousness. It is even destructive of normal, balanced mental states for, as stated above, our minds are fields of energy which absorb the subtle energies of whatever we eat and are affected thereby. To eat meat is to absorb the mental state of the animal."

In the Ayurveda and yogic traditions, foods are classified into three categories, a classification that was created as a guide to both physical and spiritual health.

Rajas – Fiery, stimulating foods and beverages such as hot spices, sugar, chocolate, coffee, alcohol, garlic, and hallucinogenic drugs.

Sattva – The pure, pristine force acting as a balance between opposite extremes. Foods in this category promote peace of mind, tranquility and optimal conditions in the body for deep, still, and profound meditation. The foods in this category include brown rice, barley, millet, and other whole grains, freshly harvested organic vegetables, beans, sea vegetables, seeds, nuts, naturally fermented foods, and seasonal fruits. The overall emphasis is on cooked, whole, plant-based foods rich in complex carbohydrates with a naturally sweet and gentle taste and ease of digestion.

Tamas – Heavy dulling foods that cause stagnation and blockage in the mind and body, weak energy in the chakras and meridians, hardening of the skin and internal organs, and degeneration of the brain and nervous system. They include meat, eggs, dairy, poultry, and other forms of animal food.

That classification is nearly identical to the classification of foods into yin (expansive), yang (contractive), and centrally balanced (middle, median, remedy, remediate, medicinal), used in macrobiotics. The foods in the Rajas category match those classified as extreme yin; those classified as Tamas, extreme yang, and those identified as Sattva, the more balanced category. In nutritional terms, what we refer to as a balanced food is one that includes all of the major nutrients in a harmonious proportion. Whole grains, for example, contain a balance of minerals, proteins, oils, and carbohydrates, in addition to vitamins. Meat, on the other hand, is almost entirely protein and fat, deficient in minerals and with zero carbohydrate. At the other extreme, refined sugar is nothing but simple carbohydrate, with no minerals, protein, fat, or vitamins. A whole food is by definition a food in which all the macronutrients are represented in balanced proportions. For deep meditation, spiritual development, and overall wellness, Ayurveda recommends foods in the Sattva category. The recommendations of Ayurveda are, in this case, essentially those of macrobiotics, and are aimed at minimizing or avoiding the importation of animal sentience. In the sacred texts of India, known as the Upanishads, we read:

> From food, verily, are produced all creatures—whatsoever dwell on earth. By food alone, furthermore, do they live. From food all creatures are born; by food, when born, they grow. Verily, different from this, which consists of the essence of food, but within it, is another self, which consists of the vital breath [prana]. By this the former is filled. This too has the shape of a man. Like the human shape of the former is the human shape of the latter. –Taittriya Upanishad

In his book, *Chakras and Meridians* (IMI Press, 2018), macrobiotic educator Michio Kushi offers a clue to deciphering this passage. Michio describes the human energy form, comprised of chakras, meridians, meridian branches, and cells ("another self, the vital breath") as an invisible tree comprised of pure energy originating in the cosmos. That energy descends from heaven to Earth. Our physical body ("this which consists of the essence of food") is formed in the opposite manner. The body is comprised of minerals, proteins, fats, water, and air arising from elements found on Earth. These elements continually replenish and enliven the body through food, drink, and breath, and are distributed throughout the body via the bloodstream. The interface between blood, which produces and nourishes the physical body, and energy, creates human life. We exist as a matrix that fuses visible and invisible, body and consciousness, matter and spirit. The Upanishads further elaborate on the relationship between food and spirit:

Food when eaten becomes threefold. What is coarsest in it becomes feces, what is medium becomes flesh, and what is subtlest becomes mind. Water when drunk becomes threefold. What is coarsest in it becomes urine, what is medium becomes blood and what is subtlest becomes prana.

The mind, my dear, consists of food, the prana, of water. That, my dear, which is the subtlest part of the curds rises, when they are churned and becomes butter. In the same manner, my dear, that which is the subtlest part of the food that is eaten rises and becomes mind. The subtlest part of the water that is drunk rises and becomes prana. Thus, my dear, the mind consists of food, the prana consists of water.

Now is described the discipline for inner purification by which self-knowledge is attained: When the food is pure, the mind becomes pure. When the mind is pure, the memory [*smriti*—memory of our eternal self] becomes firm. When the memory is firm, all ties are loosened. – Chandogya Upanishad

The following story, told by Michelle Reynolds, a registered nurse and graduate of the International Macrobiotic Institute (IMI), offers a modern parable on the way in which food influences our physical and energetic body. In Michelle's case, the excessive intake of a particular type of animal food led her to experience acute physical and mental symptoms. Although extreme, her example serves as a cautionary tale. It also illustrates how changing one's diet can change one's physical and energetic health and wellbeing.

> Around 2012 I moved from Wisconsin to Duluth, [Minnesota] to be with my husband where he works. You can imagine the excitement of being in a new town, no kids and a lot of time on our hands. At first, we lived in an apartment, which was so boring. To fill that boredom, we often went to several local breweries to try out the latest beers and have dinner. We did this several times a week, the other days we usually ate leftovers. When we were dining out, I ate mostly Cuban pork sand-wiches. If I wasn't eating pork, I was eating Juicy Lucy burgers, which are burgers stuffed with several kinds of cheese. And don't forget the fries, onion rings, and cheese curds dipped in ranch dressing.
>
> When we bought our house, we bought a grill and a smoker to go along with it. My husband grilled frequently. His favorite was to grill a pork loin that was marinated in a coffee rub and wrapped in bacon dipped in barbeque sauce. We were having such a great time with our newfound freedom when, in 2016, I started to develop several unusual symptoms. –Michelle Reynolds, Presentation at the 2018 Macrobiotic Summer Conference

Michelle's symptoms included hives appearing all over her body, a skin rash on the arms and face, insomnia, stomach pain and acid reflux, and fatigue. During that period, she also suffered restless leg syndrome, or RLS. As she describes it: "I would lie in bed and my calves would literally jump. I could put my hand on my calf and feel my muscles rapidly jumping and jerking." This uncomfortable situation interferes with normal sleep. The main symptom is uncontrolled twitching or movement in the legs, usually at night. In some cases, the muscles tighten. In others, they become loose. RLS is a symptom of too much energy running through the peripheral nerves and energy meridians that run up and down both legs.

Her symptoms can only be understood when we understand how the energy of food has a direct effect on our energy. Michelle ate an unusually large volume of pork. When a pig is slaughtered, moments before death, its legs begin to involuntarily spasm and twitch. The energy of the dying pig was transferred to Michelle in the form of cellular memory. Even though the pork she had eaten came from animals that were no longer alive, like footprints in the sand, the physical and energetic traces of the dead animal's memory and nerve impulses were imprinted deep within the proteins of the muscles and tissues. These energetic imprints were activated when the animal was cooked and eaten.

Michelle's intake of pork, which is dense and contractive, also caused her leg muscles to tighten and spasm, further compounding the problem. Because of this, plus the related health issues described above, Michelle stopped eating pork and other animal foods and adopted a whole food, plant-based diet. Her symptoms subsided and she now enjoys good health and peaceful energy, both during the day and during her peaceful night's sleep. By changing her diet, she was able to activate her innate healing powers, discharge pork residue, escape from dark, negative, and sick energy, and enter a state of brightness, healing, and grace.

5

MIND CHANNELS

Human, animal, and plant life exist at the intersection of two vast streams of energy. Heaven's force is coming from the entire universe, pressing in on all sides toward the Earth. From our perspective, this force is coming in. It appears to be pressing downward. It creates the perception of a flat earthly plane and a finite horizon. Heaven's force produces condensation, contraction, and density. It converges from infinity in toward countless infinitesimal points, including the Earth and other celestial bodies. In the human body, heaven's force spirals down and enters the top of the head. It animates the chakras, meridians, cells, and organs before exiting from the lower body in the region of the genitals. Meanwhile, because the Earth is spinning, it gives off an opposite force. Earth's force originates from the core of the planet and spirals outward. It is an outward, upward, and expanding force. It produces diffusion, lightness, and dispersion. Heaven's force is pressing down; Earth's force is expanding upward. Since both forces are ubiquitous and invisible, we don't see or perceive them directly. What we perceive are the objects and movements they produce, including day-to-day and yearly cycles of movement, rest, and change.

In the morning, Earth's rising energy is predominant. In response, we get up and start the day. When the sun's energy hits the atmosphere, things awaken and become active. At night, the sun retreats and the atmosphere becomes quiet and still. Things rest and settle down. Day and night, up and down, movement and rest. The cycle repeats without end. When we stand up, we inhale. When we sit down, we exhale. Heartbeat, digestion, and all of our bodily activities are animated by these two basic movements: that of expansion and that of contraction.

Energy coming in from the universe is strongest at the poles. Outgoing force is strongest at the equator. Energy spirals in toward the planet at the North and South Pole. Northern and southern polar energies converge deep inside the planet. As a result, the Earth's core is strongly charged with electric and magnetic energy. It is comprised of iron and similar metals that possess a strong magnetic charge. Due to high temperatures, these metals exist in a molten, or liquid state. Meanwhile, the core is rotating and giving off powerful energy that radiates up and out. Over eons of geologic time, the upward push forms the Earth's mountain ranges.

Mountain ranges also form under the ocean, for example, the mid-Atlantic and mid-Pacific ranges. Energy lines also appear as borderlines between tectonic plates. When these plates slip, a high-energy event (an earthquake) occurs. Energy from the Earth's core radiates out beyond the surface, producing an invisible magnetic field. The magnetic field extends out into space in two opposite directions. One portion projects in the direction of the sun, while the other extends away from the sun toward the outer solar system.

Similar patterns exist everywhere in nature. The products of the plant world receive energy and nutrients from roots embedded in the soil. Those with a compact round shape replicate the Earth itself. In squashes and pumpkins, nutrients and energy enter at the top through the stem. Energy also enters opposite the stem at the bottom. The converging forces spiral around one another and produce a hollowed out, high energy region at the center. The flesh or meat of the vegetable is dispersed outward to the periphery, in the same manner that the clothes in a washing machine or clothes drier are spun out from the center by centrifugal force.

Like the Earth's core, this central region is super-charged. It is here that seeds appear. Each compact seed carries information specific to its species. Each is a highly condensed energy center. Each has the potential to sprout, grow, and develop into a new plant, with hundreds, and even thousands, of new information-carrying seeds forming as a result. On the pumpkin's surface are ridges, which are traces of the energy lines radiating out from the central core. A pumpkin has ridges, a cucumber has ridges, a squash has ridges, and a watermelon has parallel lines on its surface. Energy comes in, creates a highly charged core, and then radiates out toward the surface. The highly charged central core is actually the chakra of the vegetable. ("Chakra" is the Sanskrit word for wheel or rotating spiral of energy.) Spherical forms have one chakra in the center, plus a north and south pole.

Not all vegetables have meridians that run from top to bottom. Root vegetables like carrot, burdock, parsnip, and daikon have horizontal, rather than vertical meridians. The difference is due to which of the two primary energies—that of heaven or that of the Earth, is predominant. Round vegetables channel energy from the Earth up through their roots, vine, and stem. The stem is connected to a vine that draws Earth's energy upward. Tree fruits such as apples and pears have stems that connect to branches, trunks, and ultimately roots that also channel Earth's energy. Thus, like the Earth's mountain ranges, their meridians radiate out from the center with a vertical orientation. These fruits and vegetables are channels of planetary energy, and assume the round shape, core (chakra), and meridian pattern characteristic of the Earth.

Root vegetables have the opposite configuration. Rather than channeling Earth's energy, they channel more of the incoming force of the universe. As this force pushes down into the Earth, it encounters resistance from the compact soil and rock that make up the planet's surface. It also comes into contact with the upward, centrifugal push generated by the planet's rotation. Such resistance causes the meridians to spiral horizontally, like the threads on a drill. Over time, the root burrows down into the soil. Horizontal, rather than vertical meridians form on its outer skin. Root vegetables such as carrot, burdock, daikon, and dandelion are also strongly polarized. They contain a dense and compact root portion, which branches downward, and a highly differentiated, expansive leafy portion that extends upward. As the roots push down into the soil, animated by downward force, stems, branches, and leaves erupt above the soil in an opposite reaction. The leafy tops of root vegetables are produced by Earth's expansive energy.

In the human body, the chakras supply energy to the body's life functions. The chakras are located along the body's central energy core. As we saw in the pumpkin, the central core is where life energy is most powerful. It is where seeds form. We can live without a hand or an arm, but we cannot live without the vital functions proximate to our core, including that of the brain, heart, and small intestine. Moreover, without the base chakra, which animates the sexual organs, we would not be able to reproduce and thus, would also not exist.

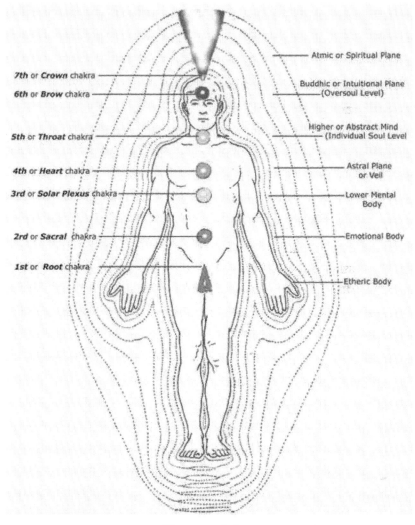

The seven chakras

The energy that radiates from our central core produces invisible lines that run just below the skin. There are twelve major lines, or meridians, corresponding to the organs of the body. Our meridians have a vertical, or up and down orientation. The human energy field does not end at the skin. It extends beyond the surface, forming layers similar to those of the Earth's magnetic field. The human energy field is especially active above the head, creating what is known as the aura. The human energy system develops in a fractal pattern. We see this pattern in plants, animals, and throughout the natural world. In ferns, for example, one stem divides into two roughly equal branches, one on the left and the other on the right. Each section, in turn, repeats the same pattern of division. The pattern repeats in smaller and smaller units until it reaches the individual cells of the plant.

The meridians run just below the skin. Obeying the law of fractal division, opposite branches appear; one extending up toward the surface, and the other branching in toward the center of the body. The branches that extend upward end in points that connect to the environment. The branches that extend inward continually divide, eventually forming microscopic channels, each of which ends in a cell. These internal branches form an integrated network, linking the body's tissues, organs, glands, and cells. Fractals appear in the brain, nervous system, lungs, circulatory system, network of ducts in the liver, as well as in the kidneys and pancreas. The human body is composed of multiple fractal systems, visible and invisible, physical and energetic, functioning as an integrated unit.

Human beings stand upright. It is that upright posture that creates a vertical link between heaven and Earth. Standing upright extends human awareness beyond the immediate environment toward the endless sky above. Animals walk on all fours. Unlike humans, their chakras are aligned horizontally. Four-legged animals also have meridians that branch from their chakras. Dogs, cats, sheep, cattle, pigs, and other four-legged mammals possess an integrated network of meridians and points connecting their organs and chakras. These channels also serve as invisible transmission lines for sensation, emotion, and self-awareness, in addition to serving as the primary channels of life energy.

Dog meridians

In his book, *Chakras and Meridians* (IMI Press, 2018*)*, Michio Kushi explains how the meridian and chakra systems function as networks of thought, emotion, and consciousness. As he states in the book:

> The meridians begin and end in the chakras. Each one is a channel for the vibrations of consciousness produced in the chakras. The body's cells are connected to the meridians through the meridian branches, and act as thought or consciousness centers. The meridians also channel energy from the environment and either activate or sedate the mental and emotional functions centered in the chakras. Mind and body are one, unified by the body's invisible energy grid.

In addition to their invisible energy structure, animals also possess cellular processes in which memory, including memories of fear, stress, and trauma, are stored in their protein structures. Sentience is not only a property of the nervous system, but is transmitted through the meridians to each cell, where it leaves an imprint in the protein molecules. When humans eat meat, they are essentially receiving a tissue transplant. A portion of the dead animal's consciousness is transferred to the consumer. We are what we eat. Thus, a person's thoughts, emotions, and consciousness are affected by the sensations and emotions of the foods he or she eats. And because the consciousness of modern livestock animals is uniformly that of suffering and unnatural death, these vibrations are consistently those of misery and suffering. These are foods of darkness rather than light.

6

Poles of Existence

Cereal grains are unique in that they channel energy not only from the immediate environment—the Earth, atmosphere, and sun—but also from deep space. In the cereal plant, the polarity existing between heaven and Earth gives rise to two opposite poles. Energy from the distant cosmos is channeled through the awns that connect to each grain. These make up the plant's celestial roots. Earthly roots are those that appear at the opposite pole, in the roots that grow down into the soil.

The two poles have correspondences in the human form. The awns find correspondence in the head hair and the seventh, or crown chakra. The sixth, or midbrain chakra, corresponds to the grains that form at the lower end of each awn. Each grain is formed through the fusion of glucose originating in sunlight, and with cosmic force streaming in through the awn. Human consciousness, centered in the midbrain, represents a similar fusion. Glucose in the bloodstream fuels the brain's daily functions, while higher consciousness and thinking are animated by cosmic force converging toward the crown chakra, and flowing down toward the midbrain.

Opposite to these celestial roots are the physical, earthly roots. In the cereal plant they extend down into the Earth. The roots absorb water, minerals, and nitrite from the soil, forming, in combination with glucose, amino acids and proteins. In the human body, this absorptive function occurs in the small intestine, the site at which nutrients are absorbed into the bloodstream. The small intestine, and specifically the small intestine chakra, represent the body's earthly roots.

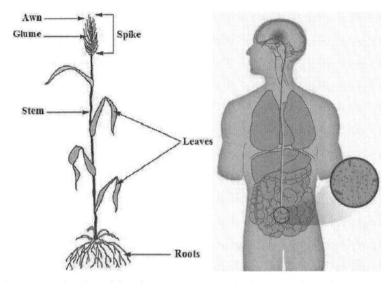

The awns and grains of the plant correspond in the human body to the crown and midbrain chakras. The roots correspond to the second, or small intestine, chakra

These centers function as the centers of intuition and instinct. The brain and nervous system are the center of intuition. The digestive system, especially the small intestine, is the center of instinct. Instinct represents awareness of and sensitivity to the world of nature. A four-legged, horizontal stance produces awareness of the immediate environment, and thus animals, especially wild animals, have highly developed instincts. Intuition, on the other hand, arises from the universe. Its source is much broader. Human beings, because of their vertical posture and evolutionary diet of awned grains, possess the seed of highly developed intuition.

Both the upper (midbrain) and lower (small intestine) chakras are at the respective centers of two independent nervous systems. The brain is dense and compact. It functions as the body's intuitive center, and as the center of the central nervous system (CNS.) The lower nervous system, known as the enteric nervous system (ENS), is comprised of nerve cells lining the expanded digestive tract. It is the center of instinct. The two nervous systems, together with their corresponding chakras, comprise the poles of intuition and instinct. The enteric nervous system is part of the autonomic nervous system (ANS), and functions independently of the conscious nervous system. The autonomic system is responsible for the body's automatic functions. When you insert the key in your car's ignition, hundreds of moving parts start to operate. These represent the car's autonomic system. As drivers, we normally don't think about these functions. We assume everything is running smoothly. What we do think about is the pleasure of the drive, stepping on the gas and braking, turning left and turning right, navigating the traffic and signals, operating the heating or cooling system, changing the channel of the radio, and other actions we take in response to sensory input or to our feelings and desires. In daily life, the autonomic nervous system is the platform, far more complex than that of a hybrid vehicle, smartphone, or jetliner, upon which we express our freedom as human beings.

In addition to the enteric nervous system, the autonomic system includes two complementary divisions, known as sympathetic and parasympathetic branches. The sympathetic branch governs the "flight or fight" response, while the parasympathetic governs what is known as the "rest and digest" response. These four poles: the brain and central nervous system (1) which is opposite to the digestive or enteric nervous system (2); and the two opposite branches of the autonomic nervous system—the sympathetic (3) and parasympathetic (4), comprise the body's axis of instinct and intuition, sense and consciousness, and awareness and automatic functioning.

The primary polarity is that between upper and lower, or the midbrain and small intestine chakra. That polarity is reflected in the polarity existing between the brain and central nervous system in the upper body and the enteric nervous system in the lower body. This vertical channel aligns our intuition and instinct with the Earth and cosmos. Like a compass pointing north, it aligns our thoughts and activities with the universe as a whole, and with the movements of the Earth within the solar system, galaxy, and greater universe. Input from this large environment is constantly being received and processed by the complementary centers in the upper and lower body. The vertical axis of instinct and intuition also governs will and judgment. We evaluate everything against the backdrop of the Earth's alignment with and movement through the cosmos, and against the sum total of vibration and energy we are receiving from that cosmos. Judgment, or the ability to see and understand clearly, is centered in the intuitive chakra and central nervous system. Will, or the capacity to act upon judgment, is centered in the lower abdomen, in the instinctive second chakra, and enteric nervous system.

These capabilities make it possible for human beings to recognize whether something is true or false, possible or impossible, and to connect cause and effect, thus making it possible to predict outcomes. The vertical axis linking the midbrain chakra (central nervous system) and the small intestine chakra (enteric nervous system) maintains our direction in life. The two divisions of the autonomic system are sensitive to the immediate environment. They produce appropriate responses and facilitate physical adaptation and survival. When the brain and central nervous system are activated, we interpret this as our intuitive sense. When awareness is channeled downward toward the enteric system, it is processed as an instinctive, or "gut" feeling.

The vertical axis of instinct and intuition, centered in the small intestine and brain, matches the vertical structure of the cereal plant. The grains and awns in the uppermost region of the plant form one pole. The roots in the lowest region form the other. Intuition is centered in the uppermost chakras and corresponds to the awns of the plant. Instinct is centered in the lower, small intestine chakra. It corresponds to the roots of the cereal plant. This vertical channel is balanced by the horizontal axis made up of the leaves. It is here that the sun's energy is converted into glucose, the primary energy source for the plant as well as for the human body, including the body's autonomic nervous system (ANS.) The autonomic system functions in the same dimension as the leaves of the cereal plant. The autonomic system works with the conscious nervous system to process sensory input and other forms of stimulation from the atmosphere and on the Earth's horizontal plane.

The vertical-horizontal axis was symbolized thousands of years ago in both spoken and written language. As Michio Kushi pointed out in his lectures, life energy is called "Ki" in Japan, "Ch'i" in China, and "Prana" in India. In Japan, the character for Ki (see below) is made up of two parts. The outer part depicts the universe streaming out from infinity and coming into being. On the Earth, this movement corresponds to the invisible movements of the atmosphere. Interestingly, the lines in the central region are the ideogram for "rice plant." They also show how the universe comes into being. From infinity, represented by the blank white page, two lines, one vertical and the other horizontal, appear. (These are referred to in creation myths as "heaven and Earth," "yin and yang," and "Shiva and Shakti.") With the appearance of the two primary poles, represented by intersecting vertical and horizontal lines, four cardinal points arise. The four again divide, so that eight cardinal stages or points are produced.

The character for "Ki," or life energy. Calligraphy by Naomi Ichikawa Esko

The process of division governs space and time. In the dimension of space, north and south represent the first division. These are the primary poles of our spatial existence. North and south then subdivide, producing west and east. These are the four cardinal directions. The four cardinal directions again divide, giving rise to the northeast, northwest, southeast, and southwest, for a total of eight. In the cycle of time, the changing of the seasons follows the same pattern. There are two opposite seasons—winter and summer—just as there are opposite poles—north and south—in the spatial dimension. The next division gives rise to spring and fall, for a total of four seasons. A similar pattern occurs in the daily cycle. Winter corresponds to nighttime, summer to noon, spring to morning, and afternoon to sunset. Each season or time of day can further be divided, thus yielding eight cardinal times of the day or year, and these align with the eight cardinal directions.

This map of time and space aligns with the rice plant and axis of instinct and intuition in the human body. The vertical, or north-south axis, aligns with the plant's vertical axis, with the awns at the top and roots at bottom. The awns channel energy from the distant universe, the roots channel nutrients and energy from the Earth. In between are the leaves, which channel the energy of the sun and planetary atmosphere. The physical roots of the human body are found in the small intestine, the primary site of nutrient absorption, while the body's celestial roots are in the head, in the seventh, or crown chakra, and sixth, or midbrain chakra. In the chapters that follow, we'll look at ways to strengthen and fine-tune the central axis and chakras so as to increase our powers of instinct and intuition, as well as the depth and breadth of our consciousness.

On a cold winter evening, my favorite place is inside cuddled up before the fire with a blanket and hot cup of tea. Here is where I unwind and relax, while escaping the blustery cold and snowy outdoor weather. As I draw nearer, the penetrating heat from the fire reaches out towards my body, sinking deep within my skin, taking the chill out of my bones. The smell of smoke disperses in the air. As I take a deep breath, the pleasant aroma calms my mind. I imagine if I could taste the air it would resemble the sweet and tender flavors of the hot tea I am sipping. I love the gentle popping, sizzling sound of the fire. It brings me peace. The bright flames of blue, yellow, orange and red dance playfully, creating a soft flicker of light in the dark room. This otherwise mundane room has been wondrously brought to life with positive radiant energy. A powerful energy that has overthrown the superficial heat from the helpless electric baseboards that line the room. Only as the bitterly cold wind rattles my house am I reminded of the subzero temperature beyond these walls. Inside this vibrant room, I feel safe. I feel warm. I am present. And I am completely relaxed.

ROBIN BREWER

It is by fire than man has tamed Nature itself.

BRILLAT-SAVARIN

Ancient wisdom is called that for a reason. Induction cooking is the new "it girl" of appliances; electric stoves are sleek and spaceship-like in design, but nothing and I mean nothing beats traditional cooking with fire. Energetically, natural fire gives us the spark we need to create life and vitality, while electric cooking feels artificial. Cooking with fire changed humanity's relationship with food and enabled the brain evolution that makes us who we are today.
CHRISTINA PIRELLO

Serious cooks including myself prefer gas stoves because they heat up quickly and give you more precise and immediate temperature adjustability.
MARLENE WATSON-TARA

7

SACRED FIRE

Each square yard of our planet receives about a thousand watts of solar energy every minute. Most of this energy is reflected back into space or absorbed and reradiated as heat. Plants also absorb sunlight. During a process known as photosynthesis, plants combine solar energy with water and carbon dioxide. Carbohydrates are the result. Chemically, photosynthesis is depicted in the formula $6CO_2 + 6H_2O + sunlight \rightarrow C_6H_{12}O_6 + 6O_2$. Translated, the formula reads: carbon dioxide plus water plus sunlight are converted into carbohydrate plus free oxygen. Glucose, a form of simple sugar, is the first food made of captured light made by green plants. Other nutrients, such as proteins and fats, are derivatives of this basic compound. The sunlight stored in glucose is the source of the energy that supports life. We are essentially light beings. In a further process, known as biosynthesis, simple glucose is used to create complex structures known as complex carbohydrates. These long chain molecules form through the bonding of smaller glucose molecules. They exist in more developed plants in the form of starch. In cereal grains, for example, starch takes the form of polysaccharide (many molecule) glucose, in contrast to monosaccharide (single molecule) or disaccharide (double molecule) sugars.

Photosynthesis and biosynthesis are both processes in which sunlight is captured and stored. The reverse process begins when food is eaten and digested. The compounds assembled during biosynthesis are broken down into their basic components. Polysaccharides, which are complex sugars, are reduced to their original form; molecules of simple glucose. Breakdown begins as food enters the mouth and continues as it moves through the digestive tract. Enzymes secreted by the salivary glands, stomach, pancreas, and small intestine are responsible for the breakdown process. In the case of polysaccharide glucose, such as that in cereal grains, digestion takes place initially in the mouth through interaction with ptyalin, an enzyme contained in saliva. Chewing is therefore essential in extracting the energy and nutrients contained in whole grains and other plant foods. Polysaccharides are further broken down in the stomach, and then completely digested in the duodenum and small intestine.

Human beings are unique among all other species. We have inserted another process in the cycle. That process is known as cooking. Cooking is a form of pre-digestion in which food is broken down and energized through the application of fire, water, salt, and pressure. Cooked food is more energized than raw food and is easier to digest. Fermentation is another human invention. In fermentation, foods are broken down or "digested" by bacteria, or probiotics, outside the body. Once broken down into their most basic form—for example, carbohydrates into glucose, proteins into amino acids, and fats into fatty acids and glycerol—digested foods pass through the small intestine into the bloodstream.

With the absorption of nutrients, the process known as metabolism begins. Metabolism involves two complementary phases. The consolidating phase, anabolism, consists of the building up of the body's substance. The opposite phase, catabolism, involves the breakdown of nutrients so as to extract their energy. Catabolism occurs at the cell level through the process known as respiration, in which sunlight stored in plants is released as heat and energy. Oxygen is the fuel for the conversion process and is provided through inhalation. Carbon dioxide and water, the elements required by photosynthesis, are given off as waste products through exhalation. Sunlight is released from glucose and waste products are produced. The energy released in this process is used by each of the body's cells and ultimately returned to the environment.

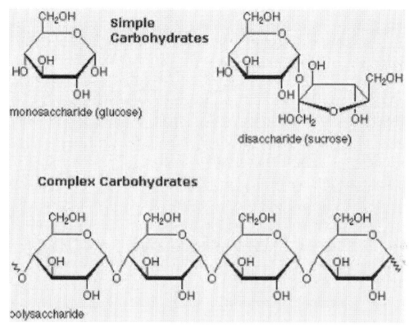

Complex carbohydrates (below) are long chains containing many molecules
of simple sugar (above.) Strong bonding force holds them together

From the point of view of the movement of energy, photosynthesis and
biosynthesis are the "capturing" phases of the cycle. Plants perform these
processes. Digestion and respiration are the "releasing" phases, and are
performed by animals. This give and take cycle is but one of the many
examples of the beautiful complementarity existing between plants and
animals. The carbohydrates in plants provide us with stored energy from
the sun. This energy exists in a highly concentrated form in the complex
carbohydrates found in cereal grains. The point of eating is to break down
these complex molecules and release the energy they contain. That energy
is used to animate all of our life functions, and especially our consciousness and thinking centered in the brain.

Just as grains and other plant foods are in essence captured sunlight;
captured sunlight in the form of plant matter is the ideal medium for cooking those foods. In one of his talks, physicist Richard Feynman described

the process in which wood catches fire and burns. As Dr. Feynman makes clear, wood and other forms of plant matter are largely stored sunlight. Burning them releases that sunlight.

The substance of the tree is carbon and where did that come from? That comes from the air, it's carbon dioxide from the air. People look at trees and think it comes out of the ground—the plants grow out of the ground. But if you ask where the substance comes from, you find out where does it come from, trees come out of the air? They surely come out of the—no, they come out of the air.

The carbon dioxide in the air goes into the tree, and that changes it, kicking out the oxygen, and pushing the oxygen away from the carbon, and leaving the carbon substance with water. Water comes out of the ground, you see, only how that getting there came out of the air, didn't it, it came down from the sky. So, in fact, most of the tree, almost all of the tree is out of the ground, I'm sorry, it's out of the air. There's a little bit from the ground, some minerals and so forth.

We know that oxygen and carbon stick together, very tight. How is it that the tree is so smart as to manage, to take the carbon dioxide, which is the carbon and oxygen nicely combined, and undo that so easy? Ah, life. Life has some mysterious force. No, the sun is shining, and this is sunlight that comes down and knocks this oxygen away from the carbon, so it takes sunlight to get the plant to work. As so the sun, all the time is doing the work of separating the oxygen away from the carbon, the oxygen is some kind of terrible byproduct, which it spits back into the air and leave in the carbon and water and stuff to make the substance of the tree. And then we take the substance of the tree and stick it in the fireplace. All the oxygen made by these trees and all the carbons would much prefer to be close together again.

And once you let the heat to get it started, it continues and makes an awful lot of activity while it's going back together again, and all those nice light and everything comes out, and everything is being undone, you're going from carbon and oxygen, back to carbon dioxide, and the light and heat that's coming out that's the light and heat of the sun, that went in, so it's sort of stored sun that's coming out when you burn a log.

In his 2009 book *Catching Fire: How Cooking Made Us Human* (Basic Books), British primatologist Richard Wrangham proposed that cooking food was a key factor in the evolution of human beings. However, the development of cooking, and the biological and social changes that it made possible, cannot be fully understood without also understanding the vital role played by the adoption of a diet of whole cereal grains. Wrangham proposes that cooking, which he estimates began 1.9 million years ago, increased food efficiency, and allowed early humans to devote less time to foraging, chewing, and digesting. At the same time, however, a diet of compact, dried grains, beans, and other seeds enabled early humans to become aware of and benefit from the regular cycles of nature and to plan their life activities in accord with these cycles. It also made possible the all-important function of food storage which allowed early humans to have a reliable, year-round source of food, independent of the success or failure of daily hunting or gathering. It was the combination of grain-centered diets plus cooking that enabled early humans to evolve in a new direction, for example, toward increasing brain size and a decrease in the size of the digestive organs and the time needed for chewing and digestion.

Wood and other forms of biomass were the original cooking fuels. They are converted sunlight and when used in cooking, accelerate the release of the stored sunlight in grains and other plant foods. In modern cooking, where wood is often not practical, the sun's energy is liberated by cooking with natural gas. The natural gas used today began millions of years ago as microscopic plants, especially green algae, and animals living in shallow marine environments. As living organisms, they captured the sun's energy and stored it in the form of carbon molecules. Dead organisms sank to the bottom of the ocean and were covered by layers of sediment. Heat, in combination with pressure, converted some of this material into natural gas. Natural gas is made up of four hydrogen atoms and one carbon atom. Natural gas is colorless and odorless in its natural state, and is the cleanest burning fossil fuel.

The overwhelming majority of professional and whole food chefs prefer natural gas cooking. Gas cooking is highly compatible with a lightfood diet. Gas stove burners are made up of a burner assembly attached to a small gas valve that connects to the main gas line. A gas burner is simply a hollow metal disk with holes in its perimeter. A gas or electric pilot light is located at one side of the burner and conveys a small flame or spark that ignites a mixture of gas and oxygen as it flows through the holes. When you turn the knob to a higher heat setting, the flow of gas and oxygen from the air is increased and the flame enlarges. Gas burners are fueled by either natural gas or propane, both hydrocarbons. Their hydrogen content gives the flame a bluish color. Yellow or orange indicate the presence of oxygen, while orange is a sign of unburned carbon.

With a gas stove, the cook can change temperatures instantly. The degree of control is unparalleled; one can move from high to low heat with the turn of a knob. Gas stoves also provide an easily controllable open flame for roasting, browning, and stir-frying, such as in a round-bottom wok. In an article titled, "Top chefs flock to the flame," published in December 2019 by the Canadian Energy Center (canadianenergycentre.com), a number of top chefs and restaurant owners stated their preference for gas cooking.

Home economist Marilyn Smith, author of eight cookbooks including the best-selling *Peace, Love, and Fibre*, says the first thing she did when she moved into her Toronto home was put in a gas stove. "There is this symbiotic chemistry that happens when I cook with gas—the stove and I become one," she says. "I control the heat and I like that there is no dial telling me it's at medium when I know that's clearly not the case." When Smith has to use the occasional electric element during TV appearances, she says timing is always an issue. "When you have only five minutes between segments to set up, electric stoves never heat up in time and I'll have to tell my producers I can't go live yet because there isn't even a sizzle."

With a chef's penchant for control in the kitchen, it's no surprise that natural gas is the restaurant industry standard across the country. "I'd say gas is the fuel of choice for most chefs in Canada, if not the world," says Luc Erjavec, vice-president, Atlantic Canada at Restaurants Canada, the national, not-for-profit association representing 35,000 restaurants, bars and hotels. Erjavec says he's never met a chef who wouldn't prefer to work with gas. In creating delicious foods, Erjavec says chefs pay close attention to specific pots and pans that perform best on gas elements. "Woks with their rounded bottoms heat better on a gas stove, and copper pots shouldn't be used on induction or electric stoves at all or they'll tarnish," he says. "That's why when you start to talk about alternatives to gas and the types of pans that need to be used, it's a big limiting factor for chefs."

In an article published in the Vancouver *Sun* (October 4, 2013) entitled, "Pro chefs always choose gas," other expert chefs commented on their preference for gas cooking:

When trying to please hordes of hungry filmgoers and celebs, the last thing a chef wants is to have to compromise his cooking methods. But that's the situation that confronted Vikram Vij during the 2013 Toronto Film Festival. "I had to cook on radiant heat because they won't allow open flames," said the chef, famous for his Indian cooking and celebrated Vancouver restaurant Vij's. "It was terrible. It was taking so long." Radiant elements are located below a ceramic stovetop. Rather than the instant flame of a gas range, the element heats up gradually, like the classic electric coil stove element. "With radiant heat, you have to have the right pan and the right pot," Vij said. As a result, his recent culinary adventure at TIFF was, at times, a disaster, he says. "It took more than two hours just to figure out what pans to use." There's a reason nearly all professional chefs prefer gas over electric. The flame heats the sides, as well as the bottom of pans, which cooks the food faster. And a gas flame allows cooks to gauge, and almost precisely and instantly adjust the heat by altering the flame.

Natural gas is the restaurant industry standard, Rueben Major says, "because it is so easy to control." Major is the director of culinary and bar development at the Earl's restaurant chain. "If you are using electric heat, like a coil burner at home, it's very difficult to control," Major said. "If you turn it off, it stays hot. If you turn it on from cold, it takes a few minutes to heat up. In the restaurant industry it's about speed. Being able to control the heat is the main thing. With the heat cutting off immediately when the flame is turned off, food can rest on the stove without continuing to cook, something you can't do with an electric range. At home, Major has a gas range. "In fact, the last two places I've bought have both been gas," he said. "Being a chef, it's one of the most important things to me. I don't know what I'd do if I had to use electric burners." For most professional chefs, there just is no alternative to cooking with open flame. "Even in India when we were growing up, it was always natural heating," Vij said. "Fire was what we cooked with. It's not the fact that it's just gas, but it's fire."

Most electric burners are coil style. They are a flattened spiral of electrical wire covered in metal that heats up when the knob is turned on, which allows electricity to flow into the wire. In smooth electric stovetops, the coils are positioned beneath a sheet of glass-ceramic material covering the stove. The electric coils radiate heat into the glass, which distributes it into pots and pans. Induction stovetops are also powered by electricity. However, in induction stoves, heat is generated in the pan itself, not in the heating element. The element beneath the glass or ceramic surface acts like a powerful magnet. The magnetic field causes electrons in pots to vibrate at a rapid rate and produce an electric current that quickly generates heat. The heat is controlled with a knob on the stove that raises or lowers the strength of the magnetic field.

The objections to electric and induction stoves are based mostly on their inconvenience. They miss the deeper energetic implications of these artificial methods. As we saw above, the main objection on the part of professional chefs to electric stoves is their poor heat control. The heating elements are sluggish and unresponsive in comparison to those on a gas stove. A gas flame is basically an extension of the cook's fingertips, with immediate and spontaneous responses based on his or her real time judgement of the needs of each dish as it is being prepared. Cooking is like playing a finely-tuned instrument in which the strings become extensions of the artist's fingertips. Sluggish responses and mechanical delays ruin the composition and the performance. Induction heating requires cookware that is high in iron, which is magnetic, including cast iron or high-iron stainless steel. Non-magnetic copper, glass, earthenware, stoneware, and low-iron stainless pots won't work. Induction cooking rules out a method of cooking common throughout Asia, Africa, India, and South America known as "hot pot," in which a variety of ingredients are cooked together in a clay pot, known in Japan as do-nabe.

The energy in a gas stove originates in the sun. A dense metal generator (right) is the source of the energy for electric and induction stoves, which duplicates the dark and comparatively limited energy at the Earth's core

Heating elements that utilize electricity, including electric and induction stoves, are based on the opposite principle to cooking on a flame. The energy of fire or a gas flame is the radiant energy of the universe itself. Light rays are generated by our sun and by an unaccountable number of stars and galaxies in the universe. It is this free and unlimited radiance that is captured and stored in plant foods and the original biomass cooking fuels. This radiant light animates not only our physical bodies, but also our consciousness and spirit. The origin of the electricity utilized in electric heat comes from an opposite dimension. The Earth's magnetic field is thought to be generated deep within the planet's core. At the center of the Earth is a solid inner core, about 65% the size of the moon and made up mostly of iron. The inner core is believed to be very hot, 5,700 degrees centigrade, and kept in a solid form by high pressure deep within the Earth. An outer core, 2,000 km thick and made up of iron, nickel, and other metals surrounds the inner core. Lower pressures cause the metals to exist as liquids. Upward and downward movements of the liquid metals in combination with swirling spiral whirlpools caused by the planet's rotation generate electric currents which in turn produce magnetic fields, in an ongoing process known as the geodynamo. Their combined effect adds up to produce one vast magnetic field surrounding the planet.

Manmade electric generators duplicate this process, albeit on a much smaller scale. According to Wikipedia:

> The operating principle of electromagnetic generators was discovered by Michael Faraday. The principle is that an electromotive force is generated in an electrical conductor which encircles a varying magnetic flux. He also built the first electromagnetic generator using a copper disc rotating between the poles of a horseshoe magnet. It produced a small DC voltage.

Modern turbines operate on the same principle. According the U.S. Energy Information Administration:

> An electricity generator is a device that converts a form of energy into electricity. Generators operate because of the relationship between magnetism and electricity. Generators that convert kinetic (mechanical) energy into electrical energy produce nearly all of the electricity that consumers use. A common method of producing electricity is from generators with an electromagnet—a magnet produced by electricity—not a traditional magnet. The generator has a series of insulated coils of wire that form a stationary cylinder. The cylinder surrounds a rotary electromagnetic shaft. When the electromagnetic shaft rotates, it induces a small electric current in each section of the wire coil. Each section of the wire coil becomes a small, separate electric conductor. The small currents of the individual sections combine to form one large current. This current is the electricity that moves through power lines from generators to consumers. Most of U.S. electricity generation is from electric power plants that use a turbine or similar machine to drive electricity generators.

The energy from a gas stove originates in the sun. It was conveniently captured and stored millions of years ago and is now available at the touch of the fingertips. It is uplifting, liberating, and energizing; as free as light itself. The energy that animates electric and induction stoves originates from dense magnetized metals, and is a small-scale version of the dark, limited, and confined environment at the Earth's core. Cooking on electric devices is the equivalent of having one's vital energy tethered to heavy vibrating metals. Earthbound to say the least. Current attempts by environmental organizations, such as the Sierra Club, to lobby local governments to ban natural gas cooking in future building construction in towns and cities across the U.S., in an attempt to reduce carbon emissions, are misguided at best. Not everyone is excited by an all-electric future. Professional chefs and restaurateurs, including plant-based whole food chefs, are especially unhappy at such a dreary possibility. Trying to force everyone to cook on electricity negates freedom of choice. The carbon footprint of gas stoves is miniscule compared to the carbon footprint and environmental degradation caused by the industrial food system. It is like comparing an ant to an elephant. The planetary environment, and the health of the nation, would be better served by calling for a ban on the sale and distribution of factory farmed meat, poultry, eggs, and dairy, including the processing and sale of these products as fast food. However, because many in the environmental movement continue to base their diet on these foods, it is unlikely that environmental organizations will call for such action.

The real purpose of eating is to further our consciousness and spirit. For that we need to eat lightfoods, and liberate the energy they contain with the light and heat of the sun in the form of an active flame. As light beings, we are nourished by and thrive on light.

The people which sat in darkness saw a great light…
MATTHEW 4:16

Your eye is the lamp of your body. When our eye is healthy, your whole body is full of light, but when it is bad, your body is full of darkness.
LUKE 11:34

The Book of the Yellow Castle says: 'In the square inch field of the square foot house, life can be regulated.' The square foot house is the face. The square inch field in the face: what could that be other than the heavenly heart? In the middle of the square inch dwells the splendor. In the purple hall of the city of jade dwells the God of Utmost Emptiness and Life. The Confucians call it the center of emptiness; the Buddhists, the terrace of living; the Taoists, the ancestral land, or the yellow castle, or the dark pass, or the space of former heaven. The heavenly heart is like the dwelling place, the light is the master.

THE SECRET OF THE GOLDEN FLOWER (T'AI I CHIN HUA TSUNG CHIH)

My view is that this gland is the principal seat of the soul, and the place in which all our thoughts are formed. The reason I believe this is that I cannot find any part of the brain, except this, which is not double. Since we see only one thing with two eyes, and hear only one voice with two ears, and in short have never more than one thought at a time, it must necessarily be the case that the impressions which enter by the two eyes or by the two ears, and so on, unite with each other in some part of the body before being considered by the soul.

RENE DESCARTES

8

INNER LIGHT

In addition to the external light perceived by the physical eyes, there is another form of light. We refer to it as our "internal" light. External light is the light of the physical universe, which takes the form of particles and waves. Internal light is the light of the invisible, spiritual universe. Internal light is inaccessible to our physical senses. Thus, for many, awareness of internal light is at best obscure or non-existent. The perception of internal light is associated with the pineal gland, deep within the brain in the region corresponding to the sixth chakra. Sometimes referred to as the "third eye," the pineal gland is not well understood. From antiquity, the pineal gland was considered to have mystical, spiritual, and religious associations. Before we consider these aspects, however, let us first examine some basic facts about the pineal gland.

1. The pineal gland is a small gland at the center of the brain with the shape and appearance of a pinecone. It has been associated with pinecone imagery throughout history.
2. The pineal gland is the only unpaired structure in the brain. All of the other structures are divided into two: left and right hemispheres or sections. The pineal gland is unified and not divided. It is about 5 to 8 millimeters in length, about the length of a grain of rice.
3. Unlike the other parts of the brain, the pineal gland is not isolated by the blood-brain barrier. Instead the pineal receives a profuse supply of blood, second only to the kidneys. The kidneys receive the largest blood supply; about one-third of the heart's output due

to their filtering and purifying function. This tiny gland receives the second largest blood supply.

4. The pineal gland contains rods and cones like those in the retina of the eye. In the retina, these serve as photo (light) receptors, making the retina highly sensitive to light. The pineal is located deep within the brain, so the presence of light receptors is somewhat puzzling.

5. The pineal gland secretes melatonin. Melatonin regulates the sleep-wake cycle in response to light and darkness. Melatonin is prevalent at night, and facilitates sleep. Opposite to melatonin is serotonin, which is prevalent during the day.

6. On scans of the brain, the pineal gland often shows signs of calcification, in some cases as early as two years old. By age seventeen, it is estimated that 40% of Americans have a calcified pineal gland. The incidence of calcification increases as people age, and is associated with a greater incidence of Alzheimer's disease.

7. There is evidence that the pineal gland regulates the function of the pituitary, including the regulation of hormones involved in ovulation, menstruation, and sexual function. The pituitary is often called the "master" gland.

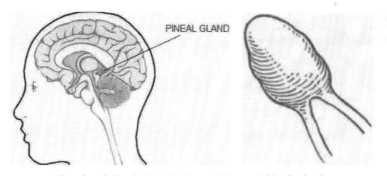

The pineal gland (right) is located deep within the brain

Melatonin promotes drowsiness and sleep. The production of melatonin peaks before puberty. It declines with age. Children produce more melatonin and easily fall asleep. Melatonin inhibits the development of sex characteristics. It declines just before puberty and with that decline, sex characteristics begin to develop. Production of melatonin occurs in response to the presence or absence of light. Sunlight during the day makes the production level decline, while increasing production of serotonin. At night, with darkness, production increases. Melatonin is calming and relaxing in comparison to a hormone such as adrenaline, which is activating and stimulating. Melatonin causes a reduction of biophotons, the light particles in the brain associated with daytime awareness.

Egyptian bas relief showing figures offering pinecone-like structures
to the rays of the sun

Throughout history, the pineal gland has been associated with pine-cone imagery. Pinecone iconography dates back to the dawn of recorded history, and is associated with religion and spirituality. In the illustration shown above, from ancient Egypt, we see figures holding pinecones in a field of light, offering them to the light. Similar images date back to ancient Sumer, depicting the special nature of the pinecone that many believe to be a symbol of the pineal gland. In Buddhism and Hinduism pinecone depictions exist, as do facial decorations corresponding to the pineal gland. On the forehead of Indian gods and saints, we see a mark corresponding to the third eye. To this day, women in India place a mark, known as a *bindi*, between the eyebrows. Many images of Buddha feature marks or spirals in the region of the third eye. Some statues show the Buddha wearing a cap that resembles a pinecone. The towers at Angkor Wat, the ancient temple complex in Cambodia, also resemble pinecones. In Rome, there is a curious statue of a pinecone in Vatican City. The birds on either side of the statue are similar to Egyptian icons, leading to speculation that the statue made its way to the Vatican from Egypt. The Pope carries a staff with a pinecone carving on top. Also, the high hat worn by the Pontiff has a mark in the center that represents the third eye. Pinecone imagery has been a feature of religious art from the beginning of recorded history.

The understanding of chakras can help us understand the pineal gland. The chakras are highly charged centers of energy. The chakras are channeling and concentrating the energy of the universe. That energy originates in the cosmos and spirals down into the planet. It then spirals out from the planet and returns to the cosmos. Energy emanating from the universe is comprised of light, radiation, particles, cosmic rays, meteorites, and other forms of physical and non-physical, visible and invisible, particles and energy. The downward and upward energies form a central core deep within the body. The chakras arise along this central line. This core is where life energy is strongest. Vital functions, such as heartbeat, absorption of nutrients, and consciousness, arise along this channel. As we move away from the central core toward the periphery, life energy becomes less vital. The pineal gland is located along the central core in the region of the sixth, or midbrain chakra. This area of the brain is highly condensed, so much so that the pineal is not divided into left and right, but is fused into one unit. Energy from the cosmos spirals into the top of the head, at the seventh or crown chakra. From there it flows downward and charges the pineal gland. From there it continues downward, creating the uvula. Energy streaming up from the earth charges the tongue. The mouth is thus highly charged by heaven and Earth. On either side are the salivary glands, also highly charged by downward energy. Thus, saliva is highly energized. That is one reason why chewing, which generates saliva, actively breaks down food into tiny energized particles.

The pineal gland contains photosensitive rods and cones. However, a type of vision that is different from our eyes is taking place there. On one hand, light from the sun and stars converges toward the pineal gland in an incoming or centripetal direction. The eyes detect that light and send it in to the visual center of the brain. That movement occurs in the form of a centripetal, contracting, inward spiral. But the pineal gland, with its rods and cones, not only has energy coming in, it also looks out. The pineal is the gateway to the spiritual universe. Vibration is coming in to our eyes from the universe and converging at the midbrain and pineal gland. Vibration converging toward the Earth becomes increasingly dense, physical, and material. Third eye vision is the opposite. It moves beyond the material universe and toward non-physical vibrations that cannot be perceived with the senses. Our vision in the physical world is created by light converging at the midbrain where it is processed as vision. Third eye vision is seeing the other way, looking out at the centrifugal universe that is moving away from us. Through the pineal gland, we are able to perceive that universe which is not visible to the physical eyes. The two types of vision, physical and spiritual, are summarized below.

Incoming Vision	Outgoing Vision
Centripetal	Centrifugal
Spiraling in	Spiraling out
From the physical universe	Toward the vibrational universe
Vibration toward matter	Matter toward vibration
Physical and material	Spiritual and vibrational
Past	Future
Fruit	Seed
Physical eyes	Third or spiritual eye
Sensory perception	Non-sensory perception
Infinity into duality	Duality into infinity

When we observe the physical universe, we are seeing the past. When you look up at the night sky, for example at Andromeda, the galaxy nearest to Earth, you are seeing light that left Andromeda 2.5 million years ago. Light reaching Earth from the sun is in reality, 8 minutes and 20 seconds old; that from the moon is about 1.3 seconds old. Looking at anything in our material world means that we are, in actuality, seeing the past. The physical universe is the world from which we emerged. The vibrational universe, perceived by the third eye, is the world toward which we are going. The pineal gland represents the fruit of the material universe. At the same time it functions as the seed of the spiritual universe, which is our future. Our world comes into being as when the oneness of infinity divides into two, creating the relative universe of transformation and change. The spiritual world is the opposite. It is the relative, endlessly dividing world of duality returning toward the oneness of infinity. These two worlds are opposite to one another. The first is perceived through the physical eyes, the second, by the third or spiritual eye.

Some people confuse the gradual opening of the pineal gland through disciplined meditation and training with the attempt to gain instant enlightenment through the use of hallucinogenic plants. Many have experimented with the tropical plant known as ayahuascha. Some have journeyed to the Amazon to participate in ceremonies that feature a tea made with this indigenous plant. Ayahuascha contains a hallucinatory substance known as DMT. Like other hallucinogens, such as LSD, mescaline, and peyote, it is an extreme substance with the potential to be damaging to one's health and mental balance. Rather than the gradual awareness of peaceful spiritual light that follows the practice of mediation, participants in ayahuascha ceremonies see terrifying visions of darkness and misery, alternating back and forth between darkness and brightness, with the appearance of terrifying creatures and beings. They need to be aware that these hallucinations are the product of their own conscious and subconscious mind, including the mental limitations caused by past extreme foods, especially animal foods, as well as the sudden violent discharge of past extremes, and not a vision of the vibrational worlds as they truly exist. One indication of the extreme nature of ayahuascha is its horrible taste, the common experience of violent nausea (the body seems to be instinctively rejecting it), and the diarrhea that follow its ingestion. The fact that people have similar visions when taking ayahuascha is a reflection of the common dietary and cultural influences they share.

Having lived through the 1960s, the ayahuascha fad reminds me of the LSD craze that swept through my generation. At that time, Michio Kushi warned of the danger of confusing the hallucinatory experience of LSD and other psychedelic drugs with the enduring quest for health and spirituality. In a lecture entitled, "Psychedelics and the Way of Eating," published in the *Order of the Universe*, July 1967, he stated:

> The difference between our attitude towards time and that of people using drugs is a good indication of the distance between us. We teach the necessity of taking time, in cooking, in learning, in development, and in life in general. When we choose vegetables to eat, we pick those that have grown slowly, suffering cold and rugged terrain, over the expanded products of southern climates that grow quickly. Those who take drugs are looking for an instantaneous way to enlightenment. In this way they are very similar to our materialistic society that promotes instant gratification. Their growth is always like the tropical plants they use to achieve this—quick, beautiful, and luxurious for a while, but finally unstable and quick to fall. Those who use drugs do so in order to be "high," but this is not what we want. Our aim is to broaden and deepen our understanding until it can include infinity itself.

An important step in the peaceful opening of the third eye is to reverse the calcification of the pineal gland; or in other words, to stop the process of calcification while at the same time dissolving any calcification that is present. The composition of these calcified deposits offers a clue as to their origin. They contain, in addition to calcium, substances such as fluoride, phosphorus, mercury, and other heavy metals. The origin of these elements can be found in the foods we eat and the water we drink, as well as in things like vaccines and medications. For example, the mercury and aluminum in vaccines often accumulate in and around the pineal gland. That is one reason why vaccines are suspected in contributing to autism. A primary source of calcification is the consumption of milk and dairy products. That may help explain the incidence of calcification in two-year old children. Children with this condition are most likely fed cow's milk formula rather than breast milk. It is highly probable that calcification of the pineal gland is less common in children who are breastfed. Stopping milk and dairy food is an important step in reversing calcification of the pineal gland.

Red meat, common in the modern diet, also leads to calcification. It is a major cause of osteoporosis. Meat-eating populations have the highest rates of osteoporosis. The breakdown of animal protein leads to a strong acid condition. Strong acids block the absorption of calcium and leach calcium from the bones. The bones become hollow and porous. Leached or unabsorbed calcium circulates in the bloodstream. The pineal receives a rich supply of blood, and is a frequent site for calcium deposition, as are the kidneys. Kidney stones and a calcified pineal gland are the common result of a high meat diet. Refined sugar also creates an acid condition that leaches calcium from bones and teeth, leading to the further deposition of calcium. The phosphorous in these deposits originates with Coca-Cola and similar beverages. That may explain the estimated 40% rate of pineal calcification found in Americans by age seventeen. A high sugar, high soft drink diet leads to the ongoing cycle of decalcification-recalcification that harms the pineal gland and kidneys. Furthermore, fluoridated water adds toxic fluorine to the accumulations in the pineal gland. Water quality is a huge problem today. It is better to avoid fluoridated or chemically treated water, and use spring, well, or filtered water. Fluoride is also added to toothpaste. To avoid this, fluoride-free toothpaste is recommended.

Together with avoiding the extreme foods and substances mentioned above, it is important to begin a grain-centered diet that avoids meat, dairy, and sugar. There is a large secret within a grain-centered, plant-based diet that few understand. Recall the unique structure of the pineal gland. As Descartes noted, the pineal gland is the only structure in the brain that is unified and not divided into two. Compared to divided structures, a unified structure is a sign of highly gathering and contractive energy. Among grains, beans, and seeds, there is a division, or split between left and right. Beans are divided, seeds are divided, and grains such as barley, millet, and wheat are divided. The only grain that is not split or divided, but wholly unified, is brown rice. It is no wonder that the arts of meditation and unified spirituality first appeared in regions of the world that ate brown rice as principal food. Because of that, organic short grain brown rice is an important food for toning and conditioning the pineal gland. Eating short grain rice on a daily basis and chewing it well, heals and strengthens the pineal gland. Here we see that brown rice, a primary storehouse of both the light of the sun and the subtle vibrations of the night sky, also serves to condition the pineal gland and open consciousness to inner spiritual light.

Brown rice can also be applied externally to activate the pineal gland. This can be accomplished by Scotch taping a grain of rice to the forehead on the point that corresponds to the pineal gland. That point is generally between and slightly above the eyebrows. It can be left on for several hours or overnight. You may notice an increased sense of calm and mental clarity as a result. All foods project an aura, or energy field. To those who can see them, auras come in a variety of colors. The aura of brown rice and other cereal grains is golden white. Photos of rice growing in the field display a golden aura that you can see from a distance. That golden color matches the golden light that becomes visible when we open the third eye.

Foods such as miso and sea vegetables help detoxify the body. They facilitate the discharge of metals and other toxins, including from the pineal gland. They can be used daily in soups and stocks. Leafy green vegetables also help loosen and dissolve hardness in the body, including excess calcium from the pineal gland. They can be boiled, steamed, and sauteed. Fresh chopped scallion, watercress, or chive can be used daily as garnish for the same purpose. Brown rice vinegar also aids in this process, as do foods that have melting or softening effects. Daikon, or long white radish is especially helpful. It can be sliced into thick rounds, boiled, and simmered (covered) for 40 minutes or so, until it becomes soft and melts in your mouth. It can be seasoned with shoyu or a diluted miso gravy. Daikon can also be eaten in the shredded and dried form. It can also be grated and eaten raw. Other foods, such as dried shiitake mushroom and unpasteurized sauerkraut help this process. Certain berries resemble the pineal gland. Raspberries and blackberries are examples. They have a sweet and sour taste. They can be enjoyed in season to help make the pineal gland softer and more flexible. Brown rice, on the other hand, has a toning and strengthening effect. Sea vegetables are good sources of iodine. Evidence shows that the element iodine blocks the uptake of calcium by the pineal gland. Sea vegetables can be cooked in soups and side dishes, and in their dried form, are especially good as condiments.

Together with a grain centered, plant based diet, the pineal gland can be activated through the direct application of energy, especially through sound vibration. Different sounds vibrate at different frequencies, and thus activate certain organs or regions of the body. Some sounds are open and expansive, while others are closed and contracted. The sound "A," for example (pronounced "Ahh,") is open and expanded. This sound is used to depict large concepts, including religious or spiritual ideas. In English, the all-encompassing term "God" is built around the "Ahh" sound, as is the word "all."

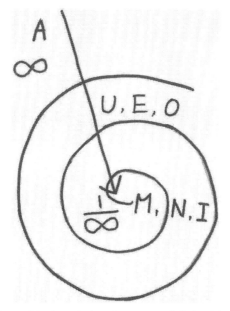

The sound "A" is outside the spiral and represents infinity. The "M" sound is at the center of the spiral and represents our highly energetic and rapidly changing life on Earth. The sound "U" is in the middle and corresponds to the vibrations of the universe that give rise to our relative world. A is sounded with a fully opened mouth; U with more contracted circular lips; and M with a closed mouth

On the other hand, sounds such as "Mm," "Nn," or "I" (pronounced "Eee") are highly contracted. Rather than universal existence, they represent individual existence. Rather than "God," we say "me." Words like "I, me, mine" are based on these contracted sounds. The sound "U" represents the universal vibration that unites all phenomenon. Words such as "universe," "universal," "unity," and union are based on this sound. The sound "AUM," which encompasses all three primary sounds, is a vibrational depiction of the creation of the universe, beginning in the infinite, passing through the universe of vibration, and concluding with the infinitesimal world in which we live. It is an all- encompassing sound, and thus has the effect of vibrating and energizing the chakra system as a whole. (This universal sound is commonly pronounced "Om.") The "Ah" sound vibrates and energizes the lower chakras, including the small intestine chakra. The "U" sound vibrates the middle chakras, especially the heart chakra. The "Mm" sound vibrates the midbrain chakra, including the pineal gland. It represents the infinitesimal world that we inhabit. Not only does this sound align the body with the vibration of the universe, it also helps energize and loosen stagnated deposits, including calcification, in the pineal gland. The chant is an important prelude to meditation in which the practitioner closes off the senses, focuses on the third eye, and begins to sense the light of the spiritual world.

Posture for chanting and meditation

To practice the AUM chant, sit with a straight posture. Place your hands in your lap, with your left hand on top of your right. Bring the tips of your thumbs together to make a complete circuit. Close your eyes and breathe in a quiet and relaxed rhythm. After a minute or two, begin to breathe more deeply, with your breathing centered below the chest in the abdomen. Let your mind relax. After several deep breathes, begin to make the sound of "A-U-M," repeating seven to ten times as you exhale. When you finish, sit with a quiet, relaxed, and empty mind, free of thoughts and distractions. Keeping your eyes closed, return to normal relaxed breathing, and begin focusing your attention in toward the pineal gland and third eye. Ignore any incoming stimulus and focus inward, not outward, not in a forced way, but in a very relaxed way. With time and practice, see if you can begin to glimpse the golden light within. To complete your meditation, slowly open your eyes and return to normal.

These simple practices—avoiding harmful foods and chemically-treated water, eating a balanced plant-based diet centered on brown rice and other whole grains, and practicing meditation and chanting on a regular basis—help melt stagnation in the pineal gland. They open your third eye and enable you to glimpse the endless spiritual realm of pure golden light.

In the beginning, God said, "Let there be light." In or before the eighth century B.C., Zarathustra, foremost among many sun-worshippers in many ages, taught the cult of the sun and the green leaf and thrift, in place of pillage and murder. In the beginning of medicine, Hippocrates, practicing at Cos in the temples of Esculapius—son of Phoebus Apollo, god of the sun and medicine and music—practiced the sun-cure. In the beginning of our era, Galen and Celsus used the sun. In the Dark Ages, by a pitiful misconception, the cult of the sun fell into desuetude as a species of pagan Nature-worship, and ill persons were treated alike in physical and intellectual night.

C.W. SLAEEBY, "SUNLIGHT AND DISEASE,"
NATURE, APRIL 1923

Nobody realizes that some people expend tremendous energy merely to be normal.
ALBERT CAMUS

9

WHEN THE LIGHTS GO DARK

COVID-19 has exacerbated the already serious problems of mental health and substance abuse. In a tracking poll conducted in July 2020 by the Kaiser Family Foundation, it was discovered that 53% of adults in the United States reported that the coronavirus has had a negative impact on their mental health, a significant increase over the 32% who reported a negative impact in March of that year. Specific impacts included difficulty in sleeping (36%) and eating (32%), increased alcohol intake or substance use (12%), and worsening chronic conditions (12%.) Factors contributing to these effects included isolation and job loss, in addition to concerns about the virus itself.

Before the COVID-19 pandemic, about one in five adults in the U.S. reported some type of mental illness in the previous year, with over 11 million suffering serious mental disorder. In 2017-2018, over 17 million adults and 3 million children experienced a major depressive episode. There was a threefold increase in the number of deaths due to drug overdose in the past 20 years, from 6.1 deaths per 100,000 in 1999 to 20.7 deaths per 100,000 in 2018. Over 48,000 Americans committed suicide in 2018. More than one in three U.S. adults reported symptoms of anxiety or depression during the 2020 pandemic. That is up from one in ten the year before.

The effect on children and adolescents has been devastating. Adolescents were already a vulnerable group before the pandemic. According to the Kaiser Family Foundation, from 2016-2018, 12%, or more than 3 million adolescents aged 12 to 17 suffered from anxiety or depression. Suicide is an increasing problem. Although suicide is the tenth leading cause of death in the U.S., in adolescents aged 12 to 17, it is the second leading cause of death. School closures and remote learning have exacerbated the problem. According to Rod Grant, headmaster at Clifton Hall, an independent day school in Edinburgh, Scotland:

> In the last three months, in my school and schools like it, I am witness-ing mental health issues unlike anything I've seen in my career. This is not me trying to be dramatic or to overplay what lockdown actually does to children. I am seeing children being diagnosed with clinical depression, increasing rates of self-harm (even in Scotland, where we already had the highest rate of self-harm in 15-year-old girls anywhere in the world, bar one), suicidal ideation and, something I haven't seen for at least 20 years, a resurgence of eating disorders. Add to this those students who are displaying worrying levels of stress and anxiety; the same students that describe online learning as stress inducing. –Rod Grant, "As a headmaster, I see children suffering mental health issues unlike anything before. This new shutdown of schools is disastrous" –RT, January 5, 2021

Depression results from the brain's inability to process the light and en-ergy of the sun. Light energy is provided internally through food and ex-ternally through direct exposure to the sun's rays. Social influences also play a role, for example, those with a cheerful outlook and hope for the future tend not to be depressed. Persons who are experiencing limitation and an uncertain future may be prone to depression and other mental dis-orders. Our mental state has a direct influence on our immune response. In the early stage of the coronavirus pandemic, for example, outbreaks tended to occur in clusters. The initial outbreak of corona was especially pronounced among groups who often lacked hope and were thus prone to depression. One such group is people who work in slaughterhouses or meat processing facilities. They experienced high rates of infection. Why do such people have little hope? Their business is the business of death. A steady stream of living, sentient creatures—cows, pigs, chickens, and others—comes in to their facilities for one purpose, and one purpose only: to be brutally murdered. The animals obviously have no hope, no future. The people who return to that environment day after also experience hopelessness and depression.

The next COVID cluster was comprised of people in prison. Prisons are crowded, like slaughterhouses, and inmates are fed a diet high in meat. An animal food diet is a no hope diet. When combined with the harsh reality of forced confinement, lack of freedom and mobility, harsh discipline and violence, the institutional diet will inevitably lead to depression, anxiety, and abandonment of hope. The next cluster was made up of elderly people in old age facilities. Institutionalized seniors may be confined all day long to bed, watching television, without natural light or fresh air. They are often cared for by strangers, often without regular contact with their families. They may be alone, having lost a spouse, and are surrounded by death and dying. Sadly, the institutional diet in senior homes is based on animal protein and refined carbohydrates. All of this leads to a loss of hope and increased susceptibility to coronavirus and other pathogens. In contrast, what age group has the most hope and thus the lowest rates of COVID infection? Individuals in that age bracket are normally in constant motion, often outdoors and in direct sunshine. The answer is of course, children. Children are brimming with anticipation and hope and have the lowest rates of COVID infection.

Regardless of their age, people eating a grain-based diet also have hope. Like other grains, brown rice, being a seed, contains the germ of new life; it thus promotes a joyful attitude and positive vision of the future. These factors strengthen natural immunity. It is difficult for a virus, which, in the case of coronavirus, is a product of bats and thus of darkness, to enter an energy field composed of converted light. The lack of sunshine has long been associated with seasonal depression and a host of physical and mental disorders. Writing in *The Healing Sun*, Richard Hobday describes the relationship between sunlight and seasonal affective disorder, or SAD:

Western literature is littered with reference to the sun and its capacity to lift the spirits. Writers, especially poets, have commented on this over and over again. Yet it is only since the 1980s that the link between light deprivation and depressive illness has been scientifically proven. Of course, the idea that sadness and despair can be triggered by low light levels during the winter months is not new to the medical profession. In the 4th century BC, Hippocrates, the "Father of Medicine," wrote that medical students should investigate the seasons and what occurs in them because of their influence on physical and mental health. Practitioners of oriental medicine have always examined the effects of the different seasons on their patients. But the condition which is now called seasonal affective disorder (SAD), a form of depression that comes on during the winter months, has until recently gone largely unrecognized and undiagnosed in the West.

Studies are hinting at the way that sunlight works against bacteria and viruses. In a June 2020 briefing, Edward Nardell, professor of medicine and of global health and social medicine at Harvard Medical School and professor of environmental health and of immunology and infectious diseases at the Harvard T.H. Chan School of Public Health stated that germicidal lamps, in use for nearly 100 years, have been proved effective in protecting against tuberculosis and are being used to fight SARS-CoV-2. The lights have been shown to be 10 times more effective than mechanical ventilation and portable room air cleaners.

> The lamps are set to shine horizontally, high in the room where sterilization is needed. Air currents, stirred in part by warmth from human bodies, circulate up to the ceiling, where the ultraviolet light kills floating pathogens, and then back down again. This technology, Nardell said, is not only proven, it can be deployed cheaply and easily in a number of settings as society requests. –Alvin Powell, "Is air conditioning helping spread COVID in the South?", The Harvard *Gazette*, June 29, 2020.

This type of light, known as ultraviolet light, is a component of sunlight. Thirty-seven percent of the light reaching the earth's surface is in the form of visible light, 3% is ultraviolet, and 60% infrared, which is the opposite of ultraviolet. Ultraviolet light has long been known to have the power to kill virus, bacteria, and other pathogens. As Richard Hobday sates in *The Healing Sun*, "Sunlight therapy was a medicine of the pre-antibiotic era, when infectious diseases were commonplace and the only defense against them was a strong immune system." At the same time, ultraviolet light stimulates the skin to produce vitamin D. Vitamin D is actually a hormone. Hormones are substances produced in the body that act as chemical messengers that control functions such as growth, reproduction, and glucose levels in the blood. Vitamin D is needed for the growth and maintenance of teeth and bones and for the healthy function of the immune system.

> It is now clear that vitamin D has important roles in addition to its classic effect on calcium and bone homeostasis. Vitamin D can modulate the innate and adaptive immune responses. Deficiency in vitamin D is associated with increased autoimmunity as well as an increased susceptibility to infection. –Cynthia Aranow, M.D., "Vitamin D and the Immune System," *Journal of Investigative Medicine*, August 2011.

Serotonin is a hormone produced in the brain that boosts mood and helps a person remain calm and focused. Exposure to sunlight increases production of serotonin. Darkness, on the other hand, stimulates the pineal gland to release melatonin, the hormone that induces drowsiness and sleep. Production of serotonin is triggered by sunlight that enters the eye. Certain regions of the retina are thought to trigger the release of serotonin. On the other hand, lack of sunlight causes serotonin levels to drop. This can lead to seasonal affective disorder. This condition is prevalent in northern regions during the winter where sunlight is in short supply.

Our bodies manage the release of the sun's energy by regulating the metabolism of glucose, or blood sugar. Glucose, or simple sugar is the product of the breakdown of complex carbohydrates, such as those in grains, beans, and vegetables. Glucose is produced through photosynthesis, the process in which green plants capture and store the sun's energy. Through the process of digestion, more complex sugars are broken down into their simplest form. Glucose enters the blood where it is transported to the body's cells and converted back into energy. Among the body's organs, the brain has the greatest demand for this energy source. Although it accounts for 2% of body weight, the brain consumes about 15-20% of glucose derived energy, in an approximate one to seven ratio with the body as a whole, making it the body's leading consumer of glucose. Glucose provides the energy for brain function and the generation of neurotransmitters, substances that transmit signals throughout the networks of nerve cells that make up the nervous system.

Understanding the way in which glucose fuels the brain becomes easier when we consider its evolutionary development. According to the Canadian Institute of Neuroscience, Mental Health, and Addiction:

> The first time you observe the anatomy of the human brain, its many folds and overlapping structures can seem very confusing, and you may wonder what they all mean. But just like the anatomy of any other organ or organism, the anatomy of the brain becomes much clearer and more meaningful when you examine it in light of the evolutionary processes that created it. Probably the best known model for understanding the structure of the brain in relation to its evolutionary history is the famous triune brain theory, which was developed by Paul MacLean and became very influential in the 1960s. –thebrain.mcgill.ca

The triune theory divides the brain into three different brains that appeared successively during evolution—the reptilian brain, the limbic, or mammalian brain, and the neocortex, or human brain. The reptilian brain is the oldest of the three. It appeared nearly 500 million years ago in fish. It further developed in amphibians and reached its most advanced stage about 250 million years ago in reptiles. It controls the body's automatic functions such as body temperature, heart rate, breathing, blood sugar, immunity, hormone secretion, and balance. It includes the main structures found in the reptilian brain, including the brainstem and cerebellum. Its functions are somewhat rigid but reliable. It is based upon protection in the moment and controls the fight or flight response. We can refer to it as the mechanical brain.

Brain evolution

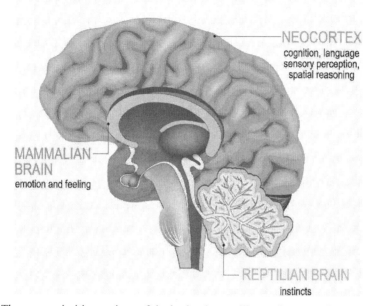

The more primitive regions of the brain, the reptilian and mammalian brain, appeared early in the evolutionary process. A developed neocortex is unique to humans and is the most recent to appear during the process of evolution

The limbic system first appeared about 150 million years ago in small mammals. Its main structures are the hippocampus, hypothalamus, and amygdala. The limbic system records memories of experiences and behaviors that resulted in agreeable or disagreeable results. It is the locus of emotion, attention, feeding, fighting, instincts, fleeing, and sexual behavior. We can refer to it in general as our emotional brain. The neocortex began its development much more recently, two or three million years ago in primates. It led to the appearance of homo sapiens with two large cerebral hemispheres that are responsible for the development of language, abstract thought, consciousness, and imagination. The neocortex is highly flexible and possesses a practically infinite range of learning abilities. Several factors played a crucial role in its development. The first was the adoption of cereal grains as a primary food. Eating grains, which stand upright in the field, prompted our early ancestors to adopt a vertical or standing posture in comparison to the half standing posture of primates. That enabled awareness to extend beyond the immediate scope of the planet itself and toward the cosmos above. A second factor was the year-round storage of cereals and other plant foods and the adaptation of fire in the form of cooking. These developments ensured a steady food supply and enabled our ancestors to spend less time searching for food and less time chewing raw plant fibers, freeing them up to pursue the development of language, art, and culture.

All three regions require glucose to function. When there isn't enough glucose to go around, certain functions begin to shut down. This condition, known as hypoglycemia, has a profound influence on our mental function. According to the University of Michigan School of Public Health:

> Many people may be suffering from symptoms of common mood disorders, such as depression and anxiety, without realizing that variable blood sugar could be the culprit. A growing body of evidence suggests a relationship between mood and blood-sugar, or glycemic highs and lows. Symptoms of poor glycemic regulation have been shown to closely mirror mental health symptoms, such as irritability, anxiety, and worry. This should come as no surprise, as the brain runs primarily on glucose. Persons with diabetes are not the only ones vulnerable to mood disturbances as a result of blood sugar fluctuations. Otherwise healthy individuals consuming a diet high in refined carbohydrates and added sugars may experience a sudden surge in their blood sugar, followed by an exaggerated insulin response, leading to acute hypoglycemia. A 2017 prospective study found positive associations between high sugar consumption and common mental disorders, concluding that sugar intake from sweet foods and beverages has an adverse effect on long-term psychological health. –Isa Kay, "Is Your Mood Disorder a Symptom of Unstable Blood Sugar?" sph.umich.edu, October 21, 2019

In my New York City lectures, I likened the effects on the brain of hypoglycemia to turning off the lights in the Empire State building at night, starting with the uppermost levels and proceeding downward to the basement. The autonomic functions centered in the reptilian and mammalian regions are the most essential for survival. Compared to these basic survival mechanisms, the functions of the neocortex are like luxury items purchased at the duty free shop. When there is not enough glucose to go around, a strict rationing program goes into effect. The functions of the neocortex shut down in order to preserve the essential functions in the brain's lower regions. The lights begin to go dark, and as a result, the person experiences depression, anxiety, confusion, and the craving for carbohydrates, usually in the form of readily absorbable simple sugars. In that state, a person can easily become less rational, overly emotional, and convert whatever circumstances they are in into a fight or flight situation.

The underlying cause of hypoglycemia is actually quite simple. Hypoglycemia results from a lack of slow-release complex carbohydrates in the diet. Complex carbohydrates form the center, or hub, of a balanced diet. When they are missing, the diet tends to extend out to the extremes. Beef, chicken, and other animal foods, which are mostly protein and fat, are totally lacking in carbohydrate. A steady diet of animal food depresses the blood sugar level and produces symptoms such as those described above, including cravings for the simple sugars that immediately raise the blood sugar level. The overconsumption of poor quality carbohydrates, in the form of refined and simple sugar, conditions the body to accept high levels of glucose. This results in the production of too much insulin, leading to hypoglycemia and its associated symptoms, including the craving for more sugar. Thus, the cycle continues. Periodic depression becomes chronic. Occasional anxiety becomes a regular occurrence. As the consumption of simple sugar continues, a decline in cognitive function may result. According to *Forbes*:

The sugar-brain connection isn't just a theory anymore. There's some fairly convincing and reproducible evidence that too much sugar in the diet is linked to cognitive and brain deficits. Two papers, both deriving data from the long-running Framingham Heart Study, bear this out. One study finds that sugary drinks are linked to pre-clinical Alzheimer's disease: Poor memory and reduced brain volume in certain areas. The other study finds that artificial sweeteners aren't much better—they're linked to a greater risk of stroke and of dementia. So it seems like we're damned if we do and damned if we don't when it comes to sweetened drinks. —"Too Much Sugar Linked to Reduced Memory, Brain Volume," *Forbes*, April 21, 2017.

The link between sugar and Alzheimer's is discussed more extensively in the next chapter. Underlying the prevention and recovery from depression and anxiety is the adoption of a plant-based diet centered on whole grains. Meat, poultry, and other animal foods lower blood sugar and cause the lights of consciousness to go dark. Refined and added sugars cause the body to overproduce insulin, also lowering blood sugar and depriving the higher brain centers. The complex carbohydrates in whole grains, beans, and vegetables help stabilize blood sugar and ease the extreme mood swings that result in anxiety and depression.

10

WHEN THE LIGHT GOES OUT

The human form is organized around two large spirals, one in the upper body, and the other in the lower body. One is expanded, the other highly compact. The center of the compact spiral is located in the upper body and develops as the brain and nervous system. This spiral system is formed by centripetal force, the same force that causes water to spiral down the drain. The complementary, expanded spiral is centered in the lower body, and develops as the elongated digestive tract. That spiral is formed by centrifugal force, the same force that pushes clothes out toward the periphery during a washing machine's spin cycle. Its physical center is deep within the small intestine. These spirals work in concert to maintain physical and mental balance. In the Vedic tradition, the center of the upper spiral was known as the sixth, or midbrain chakra, and the lower spiral, as the second, or small intestine chakra. These chakras function like the opposite poles of a magnet, or a positively charged anode and negatively charged cathode conducting electricity.

Although this relationship has been known for thousands of years, it has only been recently that modern medicine has become aware of its importance. Now referred to as the "gut-brain connection," the relationship between the upper nervous system—brain and spinal cord—known as the central nervous system (CNS), and the lower digestive tract, which includes the enteric nervous system (ENS), is coming under intensive study. The enteric nervous system, located in the intestines, regulates the complex functioning of digestion and is called the body's "second brain." It functions independently of the brain, yet both are intimately connected. "There is immense crosstalk between these two large nerve centers," states Braden Kuo of the Center for Neurointestinal Health at Massachusetts General Hospital. "This crosstalk affects how we feel and perceive gastrointestinal symptoms and impacts our quality of life." According to Harvard Health:

> For example, the very thought of eating can release the stomach's acid before food gets there. This connection goes both ways. A troubled intestine can send signals to the brain, just as a troubled brain can send signals to the gut. Therefore, a person's stomach or intestinal distress can be a cause or the product of anxiety, stress, or depression. That's because the brain and gastrointestinal (GI) system are intimately connected.

The brain-gut connection holds the key to understanding disorders such as Lewy body dementia (LBD), Parkinson's disease, and Alzheimer's. Evidence is now showing that the Lewy bodies, protein accumulations characteristic of Parkinson's and Lewy body dementia, first appear in the neurons of the enteric nervous system. This idea is not new. In 1817, James Parkinson, the English surgeon for whom the disease is named, noted in his book, *Essay on the Shaking Palsy*, a connection between Parkinson's disease and constipation. He reported that one patient improved following successful treatment of his gastrointestinal disorder. It is common knowledge among doctors that constipation is a symptom of Parkinson's. It often appears prior to the onset of shaking and other movement problems, and occurs in about 50% of those diagnosed with the disease. However, most research focused not on this connection, but on the deterioration of the brain itself. That focus was twofold. First was on the loss of neurons that produce dopamine, a neurotransmitter involved in the body's movements; and second, on the aggregation and clumping of alpha synuclein, the protein that makes up Lewy bodies.

The neurons producing dopamine, a more expansive substance, are suppressed when a person consumes too much animal food and salt, both of which have the opposite, or highly contractive effects. Clumping and aggregation of protein molecules is also an excessively contractive phenomenon, and is likewise the result of animal food and salt. However, the research focus changed in 2003 when a group of German investigators, led by Heiko Braak, proposed that Parkinson's originated in the intestine rather than in the brain. They discovered that the Lewy bodies associated with Parkinson's disease appeared in the brain, as well as in the neurons of the enteric nervous system. Further, they noted that the disease normally started in the gut and ended up in the brain.

That would seem to validate the clinical observation that in many cases, gastrointestinal symptoms, especially constipation, precede the development of Parkinson's. "Remarkably, recent reports have shown that the lesions in the enteric nervous system occurred at a very early stage of the disease, even before the involvement of the central nervous system. Besides their putative role in the spreading of the pathological process, it has been suggested that the pathological alterations within the enteric nervous system could be involved in the gastrointestinal dysfunction frequently encountered by Parkinson's patients." (Lebouvier, T, "The second brain and Parkinson's disease," *European Journal of Neuroscience*, 2009.) Researchers are uncertain as to how the Lewy bodies spread from the intestine to the brain. Several hypotheses have been put forward:

1. The abnormal proteins in Parkinson's move from the gut to the brain through the vagus nerve that links the small intestine and the brain stem.
2. An imbalance in the intestinal bacteria is at the root of the disease. Bacterial proteins may trigger the clumping of the alpha-synuclein in the intestines and brain.
3. Inflammation in the lower nervous system stimulates the formation of Lewy body deterioration. Patients with inflammatory bowel conditions such as Crohn's and ulcerative colitis, have been found to have higher rates of Parkinson's disease.

Earlier in this book we discussed the importance of the seven to one ratio. That ratio appears over and over in the fractal patterns of the body. The ratio of body to head is seven to one, as is the ratio of insulin-forming cells to anti-insulin, or glucagon-forming cells in the pancreas. The ratio of beneficial to harmful bacteria throughout the body is also seven to one. According to Google:

Actually, most bacteria are "good." Comparatively speaking there are only a handful of "bad" bacteria out there. Of the total bacteria in our bodies, a healthy balance is 85% good bacteria and 15% bad bacteria.... Many of these bacteria reside in our gut, helping our body break down food and absorb nutrients.

Here we see an important seven to one ratio with far-reaching implications for our diet and health, including Alzheimer's, Parkinson's, and LBD. The seven to one ratio reflects the ideal proportion of plant to animal food in the human diet. As we have discussed, seven to one ratio is reflected in the structure of the teeth, with 28 out of the 32 teeth ideally suited for crushing or cutting plant foods. When a diet high in animal food is consumed that natural balance is disturbed. When the volume of animal to plant food exceeds one to seven, harmful bacteria increase, so that they make up more than 15% of the total. That disturbs the natural seven to one balance between beneficial and harmful bacteria. A variety of physical and mental disturbances are thus set in motion. In the gut, this condition is known as dysbiosis. Excess animal protein can eventually lead to formation of Lewy bodies, both in the enteric nervous system and eventually in the brain. The proliferation of pathological bacteria contributes to this effect. A diet high in red meat and other animal food contributes to inflammation, thus compounding the problem. The process in which Lewy bodies form is not unlike that in which plaque forms in the arteries, leading to heart disease. Both originate in the gut.

Researchers have identified a substance in red meat that stimulates gut bacteria to produce a compound that speeds the buildup of plaque. A substance known as l-carnitine is found in red meat and dairy products. This substance is believed to contribute to the formation of plaque in the arteries and other parts of the body. In a study conducted at the Cleveland Clinic, l-carnitine was found to increase the level of trimethylamine-N-oxide (TMAO) in the blood. This compound alters the metabolism of cholesterol so that it remains in the walls of the arteries, contributing to the buildup of plaque. The researchers speculate that l-carnitine is converted by intestinal bacteria into trimethylamine, and then by the liver into TMAO, through a process accelerated by the intake of meat and animal foods.

Meat → Gut bacteria → Liver → Plaque (Lewy bodies)
L-carnitine → TMA → TMAO

Plaque in the arteries resembles plaque in the brain. Plaque forms through a constricting and aggregating process, similar to the process that causes proteins to clump and form Lewy bodies. A high meat diet predisposes not only to heart disease, but also to cognitive disorders such as Alzheimer's, Parkinson's, and Lewy body dementia. Diet either nourishes or harms our beneficial bacteria. Plant foods, especially those high in indigestible fiber, ferment in the colon and nourish beneficial gut bacteria. These foods are known as "prebiotics," and comprise the body's system of internal fermentation. Traditional societies around the world were aware of the importance of beneficial bacteria. As a result, they invented methods of external fermentation to augment the internal fermentation provided by prebiotics. Foods such as miso, shoyu, tempeh, natto, sauerkraut, and pickles are fermented outside the body from plant ingredients. Not only do they add beneficial "probiotics" to the gut, they aid in the fermentation of the indigestible fiber in plant foods.

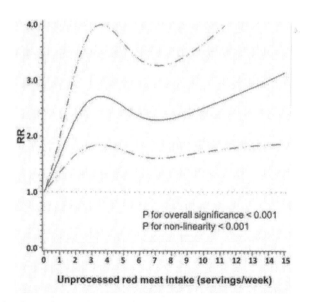

Red meat intake and gut inflammation. Statistical significance (Chan et al., 2017)

Finally, in regard to the possible role of inflammation, studies point to red meat and other animal foods as promoters of the inflammatory response. A recent Harvard study on diet and diverticulitis discovered that:

> Eating high amounts of red meat daily might be a risk factor for gut inflammation and the development of diverticulitis. For each daily serving, the risk went up by 18%. However, replacing a daily portion of red meat with fish or poultry lowered this inflammation risk by 20%. Fiber, on the other hand, was highlighted as being anti-inflammatory. Eating high-fiber foods such as vegetables lowers the chance of diverticulitis.
> –From *thehealthscienceacademy.org*

The research is varied and diverse, but the conclusions are pointing in the same direction: when it comes to cognitive disorders like Alzheimer's and Lewy body dementia, and to neurodegenerative conditions such as Parkinson's disease, as well as to heart disease and digestive disorders, the importance of diet cannot be ignored. The signs point to the efficacy of a whole food plant based diet in the avoidance of both physical and mental disorders. The digestive system is the first to encounter food and nutrients from the outside world. Next is the circulatory system, and finally the nervous system and brain. Thus, we see that, due to poor diet, degenerative changes such as those in Parkinson's, first appear in the enteric nervous system located in the intestines. Next to be affected is the circulatory system, for example by the buildup of plaque in the arteries. Last to be affected is the brain itself, located deep within the body at the antipode of the small intestine, the site of nutrient absorption.

Food → intestine → blood (circulatory) → brain

The circulatory and nervous systems are examples of fractal formation and patterning. Fractals are repeating patterns that self-duplicate from the largest forms in nature, such as galaxies, to the smallest, such as individual cells, and to all of the forms in-between. The circulatory and nervous systems are streaming fractals. They mirror the fractal patterns found in nature, including geological features like mountain ranges and river systems, as well as the structure of plants. There are two key points in the health of these systems. The first is structural integrity—the neuron networks and blood vessels, from large down to small, need to be structurally sound and able to perform their functions without breaking down. That integrity must be maintained throughout life. The second aspect is smooth and uninterrupted flow. Blood, in the case of the circulatory system, and nervous impulses, in the case of the nervous system, must flow actively, smoothly, and without blockage or impediment. These complementary aspects are maintained throughout life by diet and activity. Diet and activity impact these systems either negatively or positively, depending upon the quality of foods we consume and the type of movement and activity we pursue.

The nervous system functions like a spiral staircase. Spirals are perfect examples of fractal patterning. Impulses originate from the outside, for example from stimulation received through the five senses. These impulses move like someone at the top of the staircase descending step by step toward the ground, or the center of the spiral. Input from the peripheral nerves converges toward the central midbrain. Upon receipt and processing, signals are dispatched back out to the peripheral nerves for the appropriate response. When you touch a hot stove, for example, the sensation of heat is instantaneously transmitted to the midbrain. The midbrain signals the brain's motion centers to send the message to remove your finger. The response occurs instantaneously and without conscious involvement.

We can project fractal patterns out to the largest scale, so that we see similar patterns in the formation of spiral galaxies. We can also project fractals down to the smallest scale, in the structure and function of each of the 86 billion individual neurons, or nerve cells, that comprise the human brain. In each neuron, the central cell body receives input from the peripheral dendrites in the way the brain receives sensory input. Upon processing and integration by the central nucleus, the signal is transmitted along the axon cable to the dendrites of the next neuron in the chain, and so on, across the length of the circuit. The fractal function of the nervous system is thus replicated at the level of the individual neuron. Electrical signals carrying messages are continually transmitted in an incoming and outgoing pattern across the entire nervous system. In Alzheimer's, this basic pattern is disrupted. That disruption is due to degenerative changes that occur in the cell body of the neurons, as well as in the connecting cables, or axons. These changes progress as the disease escalates from preclinical to mild, from mild to moderate, and from moderate to severe. Additional effects are felt in the pineal gland, which we will examine as well.

1. *Amyloid beta plaques* – These accumulations, sometimes known as senile plaques, are formed through a process that is similar to the formation of plaques in the blood vessels. Intake of meat and other animal foods high in protein and saturated fat is a primary cause. Amyloid plaques form between the neurons in the brain when amyloid proteins, which normally break down and are discharged, instead accumulate, clump together, and form hard plaques. The plaques clog the delicate circuitry and interfere with the normal signaling between neurons.

2. *Neurofibrillary tangles* – Structures known as microtubules support the flow of nutrients and molecules through the axons, or skeleton, between neurons. A protein known as tau protein normally binds with the microtubules and stabilizes their structure, holding them together and keeping them intact. In Alzheimer's, the tau proteins detach from the microtubules, causing the tubules to come apart, and the skeleton to disintegrate and collapse. These are highly expansive effects. Defective tau proteins then assemble to form tangles in the neuron that eventually lead to the death of the neuron. Extremely expansive refined carbohydrates and simple sugars, especially refined sugar (sucrose), are the primary cause of these symptoms.

Amyloid plaque

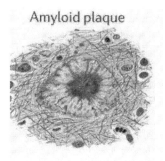

Neurofibrillary tangle

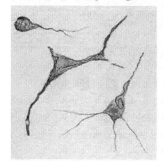

Amyloid plaques are accelerated by animal foods. Neurofibrillary
tangles, leading to disassociation and collapse of neurons, are furthered
by intake of refined sugar, grains, and highly processed foods

Refined sugar is increasingly recognized as a risk factor in Alzheimer's. Like coffee, which can have beneficial effects in slowing the buildup of plaque, sugar is a product of the equatorial zones. However, unlike coffee, sugar is highly refined and processed. Plants that grow in these areas are strongly charged with Earth's upward and expansive energy. However, in the case of sugar, the natural sugarcane plant is "refined." In this process, minerals, fiber, and chlorophyll are extracted, and the end product is an extremely concentrated residue known as sucrose. Sucrose is a simple sugar as opposed to a complex sugar, or complex carbohydrate. Sucrose is made up of one molecule of glucose and one molecule of fructose. It is the concentrated crystalized essence of the sugarcane plant. Sugar is then sold throughout the world in climates where sugarcane doesn't grow. Refined sugar is linked with many illnesses, notably the epidemic of obesity and diabetes, both of which are overly expansive conditions. In the case of Alzheimer's, the strongly expansive energy of refined sugar promotes loosening and separation of the tau proteins that hold the microtubules together, leading to their collapse and to the formation of tangles.

Studies link obesity and diabetes with increased incidence of Alzheimer's disease. Because of their predominately expansive cause, neurofibrillary tangles intially form in the contracted hippocampus, the processing center for short term memory. From there they migrate outward and upward, eventually appearing in all regions of the brain, affecting long term memory and other cognitive functions. The high intake of meat and dairy food is linked with increased risk of dementia, while a diet high in whole grains, vegetables, fruits, and fish is associated with a lower risk:

> In a 2006 study that followed more than 2,200 people in New York for four years, researchers found that people who adhered to a Mediterranean diet—full of whole grains, fruit and vegetables, fish and olive oil—had an up to 40% lower risk of dementia than people who ate more dairy products and meat. *–Nature Journal*

Animal foods are at the opposite end of the spectrum from refined sugar. They are extremely dense, contracted, and solid. Red meat and eggs are especially dense and contractive, followed by cheese, poultry, and seafood. Animal foods that are higest in dense, saturated fat are linked to Alzheimer's. As we have studied, the health of the circulatory system is essential to brain health. Patients with Alzheimer's frquently suffer from diet-casued cardiovascular conditions such as beta amyloid deposits in brain arteries, hardening of the arteries (atherosclerosis), and mini-strokes. Population studies support a connection between high consumption of red meat and other animal foods and the development of Alzheimer's. The brain is the body's final frontier. The body will attempt to neutralize or store excess from the diet in the intestines, circulatory system, and internal organs, before these deposits reach the neurons deep within the brain. That is why Alzheimer's disease is primarily a disease of old age.

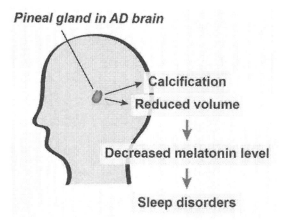

The pineal gland in Alzheimer's disease. Calcification and reduced volume lead to decreased levels of melatonin and the sleep disorders associated with dementia

It is important to note that calcification of the pineal gland, described in Chapter 8, plays a role in Alzheimer's disease. As we saw, the intake of red meat and dairy are a primary cause in pineal calcification. Calcification of the pineal limits perception of the light of the spiritual world, including the memory of our origin in the world of vibration. Our infinite memory is lost, together with more immediate short- and long-term memory. Moreover, degenerative changes in the pineal disrupt the production of melatonin, leading to sleep disorders, which are associated with dementia. That relationship is described in a recent paper published in *Molecular Neurodgeneration*:

> Alzheimer's disease (AD) is a globally common neurodegenerative disease, which is accompanied by alterations to various lifestyle patterns, such as sleep disturbance. The pineal gland is the primary endocrine organ that secretes hormones, such as melatonin, and controls the circadian

rhythms. The decrease in pineal gland volume and pineal calcification leads to the reduction of melatonin production. Melatonin has been reported to have multiple roles in the central nervous system (CNS), including improving neurogenesis and synaptic plasticity, suppressing neuroinflammation, enhancing memory function, and protecting against oxidative stress. Recently, reduced pineal gland volume and pineal calcification, accompanied by cognitive decline and sleep disturbances have been observed in AD patients. –Song, J. Pineal gland dysfunction in Alzheimer's disease: relationship with the immune-pineal axis, sleep disturbance, and neurogenesis. *Mol Neurodegeneration* 14, 28 (2019). https://doi.org/10.1186/s13024-019-0330-8

In a study entitled, "Using multicountry ecological and observational studies to determine dietary risk factors for Alzheimer's disease," published in the *Journal of the American College of Nutrition*, author William B. Grant states:

The most important risk factors seem to be linked to diet. When Japan made the nutrition transition from the traditional Japanese diet to the Western diet, AD rates rose from 1% in 1985 to 7% in 2008. Foods protective against AD include fruits, vegetables, grains, low-fat dairy products, legumes, and fish, whereas risk factors include meat, sweets, and high-fat dairy products...A new ecological study was conducted using AD prevalence from 10 countries (Brazil, Chile, Cuba, Egypt, India, Mongolia, Nigeria, Republic of Korea, Sri Lanka, and the United States) along with dietary supply data 5, 10, and 15 years before the prevalence data. Dietary supply of meat or animal products less milk 5 years before AD prevalence had the highest correlations with AD prevalence in this study. Thus, reducing meat consumption could significantly reduce the risk of AD as well as of several cancers, diabetes mellitus type 2, stroke, and, likely, chronic kidney disease...Diets high in grains, fruits, vegetables, and fish are associated with reduced risk of AD, but these factors cannot counter the effects of meat, eggs, and high-fat dairy.

Clearly, diet plays a crucial role in Alzheimer's and other cognitive disorders. A whole food plant-based diet may be the most direct way to ensure that old people stay healthy so as to enjoy their most precious memories. A plant-based diet that avoids processed foods and is centered on whole grains can help ensure that the light of memory and consciousness is not lost to the darkness but shines brightly throughout life.

11

ENERGY OUT OF CONTROL

When whole grains and other complex carbohydrate foods comprise the mainstay of the diet, the sun's energy gradually enters the bloodstream, and from there it enters and powers the body's cells. The digestion and slow steady release of carbohydrate does not overwhelm the pancreas, the organ that regulates blood sugar levels. Regulation is achieved through the production of insulin. However, when whole grains are refined, for example, brown into white rice, or when the sucrose is extracted from an indigenous plant such as sugar cane, the energy of the sun is no longer balanced by the minerals, proteins, vitamins, and oils contained in the outer bran layer. Such unbalanced foods tax the pancreas and diminish its ability to produce insulin, the hormone that lowers blood sugar by facilitating its entry into the cells. The sun's energy stored in carbohydrate enters the bloodstream too quickly, with potentially disastrous consequences. The combination of refined white rice and refined sugar (sucrose) is especially problematic.

The pancreas is a flat organ located below the stomach on the left side of the body. In its structure, function, and energy it is complementary to the liver, the large organ located opposite it on the right side. The pancreas is lower in position and flatter than the liver. The liver is large and expanded. The pancreas is animated primarily by heaven's force flowing down toward the Earth. This contractive force is stronger on the left side of the body. The descending colon is evidence of its influence. The liver, on the other hand, receives strong upward energy. This expansive force originates with the rotation of the Earth and is stronger on the right side. Hence the ascending

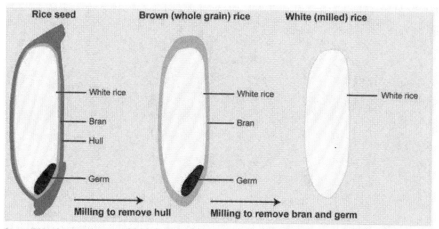

Source: GAO adaptation of image from Riceland Foods. | GAO-18-199

The carbohydrate in brown rice (center) is tightly contained in an outer coat
of bran. Refining the grain removes the outer coat and the germ, leaving
the inner carbohydrate exposed. As a result, glucose rapidly enters the
bloodstream, causing the blood sugar level to spike and contributing to the
conditions known as metabolic syndrome, including type 2 diabetes

Insulin & Glucagon are synthesized in pancreatic islet cells

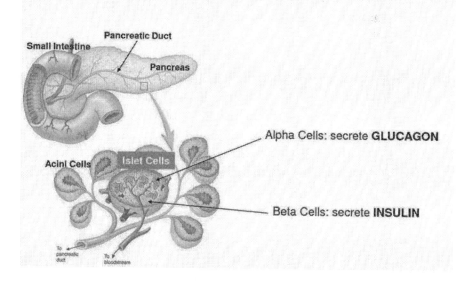

colon is located on the right. This background is helpful when understanding the cause of a metabolic disorder such as type 2 diabetes.

The pancreas performs a dual function. The acinar cells secrete digestive enzymes, similar to saliva. Pancreatic digestive juice is strongly alkaline. It especially aids in the digestion of fats. Scattered throughout the pancreas are about a million cell clusters known as the "islets of Langerhans." The islets are a compact collection of endocrine cells that secrete the hormones that regulate the conversion of sugar into energy and hence the level of sugar in the blood. The two primary endocrine cells are known as alpha cells and beta cells. The smaller and denser beta cells secrete the contractive hormone insulin, which lowers blood sugar. Alpha cells, which are larger and more expanded, secrete the expansive hormone glucagon, which has the effect of raising the level of sugar in the blood. As we saw above, on the whole the pancreas is a contracted organ. Thus, the pancreas contains far more contractive beta cells than alpha cells. The ratio of beta cells to alpha cells is approximately 85% to 15%, or about seven parts beta to one part alpha.

Insulin and glucagon offer a perfect example of complementary balance. When blood sugar becomes elevated, the beta cells secrete insulin. Insulin causes glucose to enter the body's cells, thus lowering the blood sugar level. It also signals the liver to bind glucose molecules for storage in the form of glycogen. The net result is a decrease in blood glucose. Conversely, when the glucose level becomes low, the alpha cells secrete glucagon. This hormone signals the liver to break stored glycogen down into free glucose, thus raising blood sugar levels.

The mechanism by which insulin facilitates the entry of glucose into the body's cells can be understood in terms of attraction and repulsion. Cells consist of an outer cell membrane and an inner cell nucleus. Free glucose circulating in the blood has the opposite polarity from insulin. Glucose, which is expansive, is naturally repelled by the expansive cell membrane; it needs a contractive agent to facilitate transfer through the membrane and into the interior of the cell. This is accomplished by insulin. Insulin readily bonds with receptors on the cell membrane and passes through the membrane into the interior. The presence of insulin below the surface membrane changes the quality of the membrane. It now reverses polarity and attracts and admits glucose. Diabetes occurs when the pancreas either does not produce enough insulin or when the body's cells resist or reject the insulin that is produced. The result is high blood sugar, or hyperglycemia, which produces a number of symptoms and side effects, both immediate and long term.

Modern medicine remains powerless in the face of the planet-wide surge in diabetes. In a special 200th anniversary article in the *New England Journal of Medicine* (*NEJM* 2012; 367-1332/October 4, 2012) entitled "The Past 200 Years in Diabetes," Dr. Kenneth Polonsky stated: "…The pathway to cure has remained elusive. In fact, if one views diabetes from a public health and overall societal standpoint, little progress has been made toward conquering the disease during the past 200 years, and we are arguably worse off now than we were in 1812." Could it be that after billions in research and decades of effort, we are worse off now than we were two centuries ago?

In his article Dr. Polonsky describes the disease as follows:

Over the past two centuries, we have learned that diabetes is a complex, heterogeneous disorder. Type 1 diabetes occurs predominantly in young people and is due to selective autoimmune destruction of the pancreatic beta cell, leading to insulin deficiency. Type 2 diabetes is much more common, and the vast majority of people with this disorder are overweight. The increase in body weight in the general population, a result of high-fat, high-calorie diets and a sedentary lifestyle, is the most important factor associated with the increased prevalence of type 2 diabetes. Older adults are most likely to have type 2 diabetes, although the age at onset has been falling in recent years. Type 2 diabetes is now common among teenagers and young adults. We now know that insulin resistance is essential in the pathogenesis of type 2 diabetes, and that the disease results from both insulin resistance and impaired beta cell function.

Both insulin resistance and impaired beta cell function are expansive conditions, as are obesity and overweight. A primary cause of these conditions is the intake of strongly expansive simple sugars, such as refined sugar, as well as refined carbohydrates like white rice and white flour. The continual intake of extremes exhausts and depletes the beta cells. The result is either not enough insulin or insulin that is too weak to facilitate the transfer of glucose across the cell membrane. If insulin lacks strong contractive power, it will not be able to bond with the cell membrane and enter the interior of the cell. Without insulin as a facilitator, glucose does not enter the cell but remains circulating in the blood, hence the high level of blood glucose characteristic of diabetes. This mechanism explains the onset of type 2 diabetes.

The mechanism of type 1 diabetes is a little different, albeit also caused by extreme diet. T. Colin Campbell, PhD in *The China Study*, best describes the process:

This devastating, incurable disease strikes children, creating a painful and difficult experience for young families. What most people don't know, though, is that there is strong evidence that this disease is linked to diet and, more specifically to dairy products. The ability of cow's milk protein to initiate type 1 diabetes is well documented.

In some infants, cow milk proteins are not fully digested and small amino acid chains or protein fragments are absorbed by the small intestine. In the bloodstream the immune system identifies these fragments as antigens, or foreign proteins, and codes antibodies to destroy them. Some of these protein fragments are similar in form to insulin-producing beta cells. Antibodies produced by the immune system thus destroy both the cow proteins and the beta cells, taking away the child's ability to produce insulin. The result is type 1 diabetes, an incurable lifetime condition. Milk, a product of the animal body, is a powerful secretion designed for growth. This is especially true for the milk of large mammals such as cows. The intake of this strongly expansive substance (often together with refined sugar) is largely responsible for the onset of type 1 diabetes.

Carbohydrates come in two types: "simple" or "complex." Simple carbohydrates contain just one sugar molecule (monosaccharide) or two sugar molecules (disaccharide.) Simple sugars demonstrate strong expansive force. These molecules enter the bloodstream quickly. They cause a rapid spike in blood sugar. In the case of added sugars and refined carbohydrates, the sun's energy, stored in the sugar molecules, is uncontained and unopposed. In contrast, complex carbohydrates, such as those in brown rice, beans, and vegetables, consist of a chain of sugar molecules linked together. They are connected by strong bonding force. The sun's energy stored in glucose is wrapped in a whole food package. The body has to work harder to break down the links in the chain; hence they enter the bloodstream more slowly than simple sugars. The level of sugar in the blood remains constant and steady.

Examples of simple carbohydrates include table sugar, honey, fruit, fruit juice, jam, and chocolate. They are often labeled "bad" because they are high in calories compared to their nutritional content and because of their effect on blood sugar. Complex carbohydrates are lower in net calories and are sometimes touted as "healthy carbs." They include foods like whole grains, beans, whole grain bread and pasta, vegetables, especially sweet-tasting ones, and sea vegetables.

The A1c test is used to measure levels of blood sugar and the appearance of diabetes. The test is based on a measurement of the amount of sugar, or glucose, that attaches to red blood cells. At their core, red blood cells contain hemoglobin; a protein that contains iron and that carries oxygen from the lungs to all the cells of the body. Because of their hemoglobin, and the iron it contains, red blood cells are dense and contracted. Thus, red cells readily attract and bind with oxygen, which is highly expansive. Iron is a dense, solid, and heavy metal; oxygen is a light gas. Red cells also link up with sugars such as glucose, which as we have seen, are strongly expansive. Glucose enters the red blood cells and binds (or glycates) with molecules of hemoglobin, an example of the law of opposites attracting. The higher the level of glucose in the blood, the more hemoglobin gets glycated. Measuring the percentage of A1c in the blood makes it possible to get an overview of average blood glucose levels over the previous two to three months. The normal range for the hemoglobin A1c test for persons without diabetes is between 4% and 5.6%. Increased risk for diabetes is reflected in hemoglobin A1c levels between 5.7% and 6.4%. A level of 6.5% or higher indicates diabetes.

These levels indicate the red cells have lost their normal contractive quality and are becoming over expanded and weak.

Studies have shown that uncontrolled diabetes results in complications from the disease, such as eye, kidney, skin, and other potentially serious problems. Doctors advise people with diabetes to achieve a hemoglobin A1c that is less than 7%. Healthy A1c levels can be achieved by eliminating white sugar, white bread, white rice, and white potato, and by adopting a balanced macrobiotic diet. Organic brown rice contains beneficial fiber, minerals, vitamins, and phytochemicals like beta-carotene. Milling and polishing brown rice removes most of its vitamins and minerals. It also strips away most of the fiber. The fiber in brown rice and other whole grains slows the absorption of glucose and helps prevent diabetes. That is because the carbohydrate in whole grain fibers is yang and cohesive. The body has to work harder to break the links that bind the carbohydrate chains together.

Although the starch in white rice, white flour, and a baked potato is in the form of complex carbohydrate, the body converts this starch into blood sugar almost as quickly as it processes pure glucose. These foods cause a rapid rise in blood sugar and are classified as having a high glycemic index. The glycemic index classifies foods on how quickly and how high they raise the level of sugar in the blood in comparison to pure glucose. As we have seen, a food like brown rice is slowly digested. It doesn't cause a rapid spike in blood sugar and is classified as having a low glycemic index. When brown rice is milled and refined by removing its bran and germ, its glycemic index rises. The same is true of whole wheat and other grains. Finely ground grain (expansive) is more rapidly digested than coarsely ground grain (contractive), and has a higher glycemic index.

The type of starch is also a factor in determining a food's glycemic index. An expansive starch, such as that in potato, is rapidly digested and absorbed. Potatoes have a high glycemic index. More contractive starches, like those in brown rice, are processed more slowly and have a low glycemic index. Because of these factors, brown rice is being touted as a possible solution to the diabetes epidemic, especially in China, India, and other white rice-eating countries. A January 2012 article from the Harvard

School of Public Health entitled, "Can Brown Rice Slow the Spread of Type 2 Diabetes?" states:

> The worldwide spike in type 2 diabetes in recent decades has paralleled a shift in diets away from staple foods rich in whole grains to highly refined carbohydrates, such as white rice and refined flours. Now a group of researchers at Harvard School of Public Health (HSPH) aims to stem the tide by changing the color of the world's rice bowl from white to more-nutritious brown.

The announcement of a collaborative initiative to prevent the global diabetes epidemic by improving the quality of carbohydrate follows an earlier study published on June 14, 2010 on the website of the journal *Archives of Internal Medicine*. In the study, HSPH researchers found that eating five or more servings of white rice per week was associated with an increased risk of type 2 diabetes, while a diet that includes two or more servings of brown rice was associated with a lower risk. The investigators estimated that the risk of type 2 diabetes could be lowered by 16% by replacing 50 grams of white rice (1/3rd of a typical daily serving) with the same amount of brown rice. Interestingly, replacing the same amount of white rice with whole wheat or barley was associated with a 36% lower risk. "From a public health point of view, whole grains, rather than refined carbohydrates, such as white rice should be recommended as the primary source of carbohydrates for the U.S. population," said senior researcher Frank Hu. "These findings could have even greater implications for Asian and other populations in which rice is a staple food."

Michio Kushi and other macrobiotic educators have for decades advocated an approach similar to the approach advocated by the Harvard School of Public Health. A macrobiotic diet, based on whole grains and other plant-based lightfoods, may offer the most effective approach to the prevention of diabetes. Macrobiotics advocates avoiding the milk and dairy products associated with type 1 diabetes. Breast-feeding is the preferred method of nourishing infants and children. Refined sugar and artificial sweeteners like high fructose corn syrup are not recommended. Macrobiotics recommends avoiding or reducing foods such as potatoes, white flour, white rice, and others with a high glycemic index. Instead, foods rich in complex carbohydrates and fiber like whole grains, beans, fresh vegetables, and sea vegetables are the foundation of a macrobiotic diet. These foods are associated with a lower risk of type 2 diabetes. The quality of salt used as seasoning is also important. Mineral rich sea salt is preferred over refined table salt. Some evidence has come in that one brand of sea salt, known as Si Salt, harvested in the pristine ocean off Baja California, aids in lowering blood sugar levels.

Moreover, a plant-based diet centered on whole grains may prove an effective tool in the management of diabetes. In type 2 diabetes, successful management and recovery have been noted in persons adopting a macrobiotic way of eating. Persons with type 2 diabetes have experienced a marked reduction in the need for medication; some after only one or two weeks after beginning the diet. Some patients have eliminated the need for medication entirely, while noting marked improvements in overall health. At the very least, macrobiotics is acknowledged as an effective tool in weight loss and weight management. Patients with type 1 diabetes have noted reductions in the need for insulin and a lessening of complications after adopting a plant-based macrobiotic way of eating. Macrobiotics can help these patients better manage their condition. With the mounting evidence linking diet with the cause, prevention, management, and potential recovery from diabetes, the time has come for clinical trials of a plant-based macrobiotic approach. A grain-centered lightfood diet could very well offer a sustainable solution to this 21st century epidemic by ensuring that the energy of the sun is properly utilized in the human body.

First it was rabies, the pathogen that escaped Louis Pasteur's attention under the microscope and led him to imagine the existence of infectious agents smaller than bacteria. More recently it has been Ebola, Marburg, Hendra, Nipah, the Severe Acute Respiratory Syndrome virus (SARS), the Middle East Respiratory Syndrome virus (MERS) and, of course, the SARS-CoV-2 coronavirus of COVID-19. All these viruses have something in common: they are supposed to have come into existence in bats and ended up reaching humans. Nearly 11,000 different types of viruses are already known in bats, almost 3,800 of which are coronaviruses. But are they merely victims of a bad press or do these animals really have something special that makes them virus incubators? And if so, how do they survive? – "How Bats Can Be Incubators of Viruses and Not Die in the Process."
OPENMIND BBVA

And I heard another voice from heaven, saying, Come out of her, my people, that ye be not partakers of her sins, and that ye receive not of her plagues.
REVELATION 18

12

LIKE HELL OUT OF A BAT

There is a clear link between the spread of viruses and the reliance on animal food and the proximity to animals. According to the U.S. Centers for Disease Control, "Approximately 75% of recently emerging diseases affecting people began as diseases in animals." The greatest pandemic of the last century, the 1918 flu, which infected over a quarter of the world's population and resulted in 50 million deaths, was the result of an H1N1 virus traced to a chicken farm in Kansas. The H1N1 pandemic of 2009 that affected the U.S. and Mexico, originated in pig populations. Avian flu, Ebola, HIV, SARS, swine flu, and vCJD, all of which affect humans, originated in animals. According to PETA:

> Swine flu—which is linked to pigs—has killed thousands of people worldwide. And bird flu (or avian flu) is a disease that can spread easily on a crowded chicken farm. There are at least 144 strains of bird flu. The H5N1 variety kills the most birds and is deadly to humans, killing about 60% of those who catch it.

Modern feedlots, livestock warehouses, and food processing facilities are breeding grounds for disease. Crowded, filthy conditions allow bacteria to spread quickly. Antibiotics are given to livestock to reduce infection and also to promote growth. Animals in the U.S. now consume more antibiotics per year than humans do. This has promoted the rise of antibiotic-resistant strains of bacteria, rendering many antibiotics useless against bacterial infection. Moreover, overuse of antibiotics has a negative impact on the gut bacteria, thus weakening natural immunity and increasing susceptibility to viral infection. Meat processing facilities have become hotspots of COVID-19 infection, leading to plant closings and the possibility of meat shortages throughout the U.S. According to NPR:

> Tyson Foods, one of the biggest meat producers in the U.S., is suspending work at its pork processing plant in Waterloo, Iowa. Officials in Black Hawk County, where the plant is located, say at least 150 people with close connections to the plant have tested positive for the coronavirus, according to Iowa Public Radio. The Waterloo plant, which employs 2,800 people, is just the latest U.S. meatpacking plant to shut down or reduce production. Other closed plants include a Smithfield Foods pork processing facility in Sioux Falls, S.D., which has been linked to over 900 infections, and a JBS beef plant in Greeley, Colo. Other plants are open but operating at a slower pace because many workers are absent.

These disruptions are exposing just how vulnerable the highly centralized supply chains of the modern food industry are. Increasing consolidation has led to only four companies accounting for over 80% of all beef processing in the U.S. The concentration of the U.S. food system, especially the production of meat and other animal foods, into fewer and fewer hands is a leading example of the fundamental unsustainability underlying many aspects of modern life. The trend toward consolidation has produced an increasing polarity between extremes. On the one hand, we see increasingly extended supply chains for food, medicines, and consumer goods, while on the other hand, there has been a significant consolidation of the production and distribution of these commodities in fewer and fewer hands. The corona crisis has brought the weakness of modern systems into sharp relief. It has also highlighted the poor state of health of the American population, and the failure of the healthcare system to adequately address these concerns. The vast majority of people who experienced life-threatening symptoms were suffering from obesity or another pre-existing condition. In New York State, the initial epicenter of the epidemic in the U.S., 89% of deaths from COVID-19 occurred in those with one or more chronic conditions, or comorbidities. The top five risk factors, aside from age included hypertension, diabetes, high cholesterol, coronary artery disease, and dementia.

These comorbidities are due largely to diet and lifestyle, especially a diet high in animal food, sugar, and refined and processed foods, and are thus preventable. Rather than placing all bets on a vaccine, the medical profession should promote more fundamental dietary and lifestyle solutions. Strengthening natural immunity should become the top priority. Of course, everyone appreciates the dedication and bravery of doctors, nurses, and all front line responders in this crisis. However, the problem lies with the orientation of the medical system as a whole. The medical profession needs to become proactive by getting ahead of infectious disease, rather than remaining passive and struggling to react once a pandemic appears. Education may thus prove to be the most powerful tool against viral infection. A healthier population will mean that fewer front line responders will be exposed to such concentrated risk if an epidemic occurs.

Virus and bacteria have been on Earth for several billions of years. Humans have coexisted with viruses and bacteria from the beginning; in fact, we couldn't exist without the colonies of beneficial bacteria that inhabit our digestive tract. When humans are living, and especially eating, with respect for the natural order, and thus maintaining strong natural immunity, there is no need to fear viruses, bacteria, or any other part of the natural environment. Virus and bacteria have opposite characteristics. Bacteria are more biologically developed than bacteria. They are single-celled organisms, while viruses are non-living. Bacteria tend to produce localized infection, while virus infections are often systemic. And, perhaps most importantly, bacteria respond to antibiotics, while viruses do not.

Many viruses, including the novel coronavirus, bear a striking resemblance to World War II ocean mines. Both inflict damage if engaged. If left alone, they remain harmless. The outer shell of the ocean mine is made of metal. The inner core is packed with explosive. Virus particles contain the viral genome packaged in a protein coat called the capsid. Like ocean mines, the explosive portion, the genetic material, which in the case of COVID-19 consists of RNA, is located just below the surface in the interior. Bacteria are the opposite. Delicate, hair-like projections extend from the surface, in contrast to the spikes extending from the outer coat of a virus. The inner portion of the bacteria is comprised of a compact nucleus containing DNA in contrast to the mostly hollow inner portion of the virus. The hard spikes that protrude from the virus bond with receptors on the outer membrane of the body's cells. These are known as s-protein spikes. Once inside, the RNA of the virus overwhelms the genetic material of the cell, including the DNA at the center. Rather than serve the needs of the cell, the alien RNA causes the cell to begin replicating viruses, a process that continues until the cell explodes, releasing many new viruses that go on to infect other cells, in a continually repeating process.

Like bacteria, viruses are divided into opposite subtypes. In the case of bacteria, there are gram-negative and gram-positive varieties. Among viruses, some are milder, others more severe; some last several days, while others persist; some affect the upper respiratory passages, while others move downward and attach to cells deep inside the lung. The cold and flu viruses offer a perfect example of these opposite tendencies. The differences between the cold and flu viruses are apparent: colds are milder; the flu is more severe. The flu lasts longer, while a cold goes away more rapidly. Colds affect the upper respiratory tract; the flu goes deeper, producing a dry cough. A cold is inconvenient; the flu can be fatal for those with compromised immunity.

The animals suspected of originating coronavirus share a number of characteristics. Bats are creatures of darkness, and are suspected in both SARS and COVID-19. Bats come in two varieties; insect eating bats and fruit eating bats. The bats suspected in coronavirus are insect eating carnivores known as horseshoe bats. Civet cats, raccoon-like creatures, are also suspected. They are also carnivores. The pangolin, a form of spiny anteater, consumes ants and termites. Pangolins have also been suspected in transmitting coronaviruses to humans. All three are carnivorous—they eat insects and animals—and are nocturnal. This combination—a carnivorous diet plus nocturnal activity—may prove to be a breeding ground for a variety of coronaviruses, especially those that penetrate deep within the respiratory system. It may also help explain why viral outbreaks tend to be more severe in cold and dark weather characteristic of autumn, winter, and nighttime. The coronavirus is apparently a product of darkness and seems to thrive under such conditions.

There are two competing theories as to the origin of COVID-19. One, known as the natural origin theory, states that the virus originated in bats and was somehow transferred to humans, specifically through the Huanan Seafood Market (the "wet" market) in Wuhan that offers customers a variety of exotic animals to be eaten as food. In this theory, the virus, like SARS, originated in bats and was passed to another mammal such as a pangolin, and eventually entered the human population. The other theory states that the novel coronavirus was created in a laboratory as the result of so-called "gain of function" research, which has been conducted all over the world, and especially on bat viruses at the Wuhan Institute of Virology in China. A 2015 article in the journal *Nature* described the potential dangers of gain of function research on bat viruses:

An experiment that created a hybrid version of a bat coronavirus—one related to the virus that causes SARS (severe acute respiratory syndrome)—has triggered renewed debate over whether engineering lab variants of viruses with possible pandemic potential is worth the risks. In an article published in *Nature Medicine* on 9 November, scientists investigated a virus called SHCO14, which is found in horseshoe bats in China. The researchers created a chimaeric virus, made up of a surface protein of SHCO14 and the backbone of a SARS virus that had been adapted to grow in mice and to mimic human disease. The chimaera infected human airway cells—proving that the surface protein of SHCO14 has the necessary structure to bind to a key receptor on the cells and to infect them. The findings reinforce suspicions that bat coronaviruses capable of directly infecting humans (rather than first needing to evolve in an intermediate animal host) may be more common than previously thought, the researchers say. But other virologists question whether the information gleaned from the experiment justifies the potential risk. Simon Wain-Hobson, a virologist at the Pasteur Institute in Paris, points out that the researchers have created a novel virus that "grows remarkably well" in human cells. "If the virus escaped, nobody could predict the trajectory," he says. –Declan Butler, "Engineered bat virus stirs debate over risky research" –*Nature*, November 12, 2015.

According to some observers, that is precisely what happened with COVID-19. The artificial origin theory points to the fact that the Wuhan Institute of Virology has, since 2005, been conducting research on the horseshoe bat as the source of SARS-like coronaviruses, including gain of function experiments. The artificial origin theory states that an enhanced coronavirus escaped from the Wuhan lab, resulting in the corona epidemic. As of this writing, the origin of COVID-19 remains uncertain. According to *Newsweek*:

For one thing, the Wuhan Institute of Virology, not far from the animal markets in downtown Wuhan, houses the world's largest collection of coronaviruses from wild bats, including at least one virus that bears a resemblance to SARS-CoV-2. What's more, Wuhan Institute of Virology scientists have for the past five years been engaged in so-called "gain of function" (GOF) research, which is designed to enhance certain properties of viruses for the purpose of anticipating future pandemics. Gain-of-function techniques have been used to turn viruses into human pathogens capable of causing a global pandemic. –"The Controversial Experiments and Wuhan Lab Suspected of Starting the Coronavirus Epidemic," –*Newsweek*, April 27, 2020.

In a healthy individual, the immune system prevents viruses from infecting cells and causing damage. Viruses are neutralized by specialized cells of the immune system, including cytotoxic T cells and natural killer cells (NK cells) that destroy infected cells, as well as through the production of antibodies. In one such process, antibodies cause virus particles to stick together, making them easier targets for immune cells than single particles. In another process, known as phagocytosis, phagocyte cells are activated by antibodies, triggering a process by which the phagocyte cell engulfs and destroys the virus.

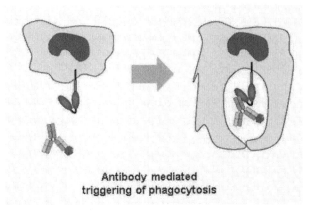

**Antibody mediated
triggering of phagocytosis**

The antibody actives the phagocyte cell (top) to engulf the virus (bottom)

As we can see, the health of the immune system is vital in protecting the body from potentially harmful viruses. Much of the body's immune response occurs within the digestive tract. According to some estimates, the gut wall is home to 70 to 80 % of the cells that comprise the immune system. Together with breaking down food and absorbing and producing nutrients, the digestive tract plays a vital role in the body's immune response. According to Andrew M. Platt of the University of Glasgow:

> The large intestine (colon) has a large resident population of microbes, consisting of at least 10^{12} organisms per gram of luminal contents. These organisms, together with the antigenic load provided by the diet and the constant threat of potential pathogens, means the intestinal immune system encounters more antigen than any other part of the body.

The fact that a large proportion of coronavirus infections begin with digestive symptoms suggests that the intestinal immune system plays an important role in the development of the disease. In a study published in March 2020 in the *American Journal of Gastroenterology*, Chinese researchers examined data from 204 patients in Hubei province, believed to be the geographical center of the 2019 outbreak. Of these patients, 99 (48.5%) went to the hospital with one or more digestive symptoms as their major complaint. Symptoms included diarrhea, vomiting, and abdominal pain.

According to the researchers, "Of these 99 patients, 92 developed respiratory symptoms along with digestive symptoms, and seven presented with only digestive symptoms in the absence of respiratory symptoms. Among the 105 patients without digestive symptoms, 85 presented only with respiratory symptoms, and 20 neither had respiratory nor digestive symptoms as their chief complaint." Digestive issues were not only a first sign of illness, but also those who reported them tended to become sicker than those who did not. "Moreover, as the severity of the disease increased, digestive symptoms became more pronounced. Patients without digestive symptoms were more likely to be cured and discharged at the time of this study than patients with digestive symptoms." The researchers noted that 60% of patients with no digestive symptoms recovered, compared to 34% of those suffering from digestive symptoms. They further stated that, "Clinicians must bear in mind that digestive symptoms, such as diarrhea, may be a presenting feature of COVID-19 that arise before respiratory symptoms, and on rare occasions are the only presenting symptom of COVID-19."

Researchers at the Renmin Hospital of Wuhan University and the Wuhan Institute of Virology of the Chinese Academy of Science reported in February 2020 that the coronavirus might be transmitted through the digestive tract. They found genetic material of the virus in stool samples from patients, leading them to propose that the novel coronavirus may be spread through the fecal-oral route, as well as through droplets inhaled by the respiratory system. This is one among many findings linking the condition of the lower digestive tract, especially the large intestine, with the lung and respiratory system. This relationship is mediated by the microbiome, the vast colonies of bacteria, most of which are beneficial, that inhabit the digestive tract. An article by Helen Fields published by Johns Hopkins in March 2020, entitled, "The Gut: Where Bacteria and Immune System Meet," states that a "huge proportion of your immune system is actually in your G.I. tract."

Although gut bacteria influence the body's overall immune response, their relationship to the lung is especially relevant to respiratory infections. The connection between the large intestine and lung is referred to as the "gut-lung" axis. In a paper by researchers Anh Thu Dang and Benjamin J.

Edward Esko

Marsland, appearing in the journal *Mucosal Immunology* in April 2019, the gut-lung axis is explained as follows:

> The microbiota plays an essential role in the education, development, and function of the immune system, both locally and systemically. Emerging experimental and epidemiological evidence highlights a crucial cross-talk between the intestinal microbiota and the lungs, termed the 'gut-lung axis.' Changes in the constituents of the gut microbiome, through diet, disease or medical interventions (such as antibiotics) is linked with altered immune responses and homeostasis in the airways.

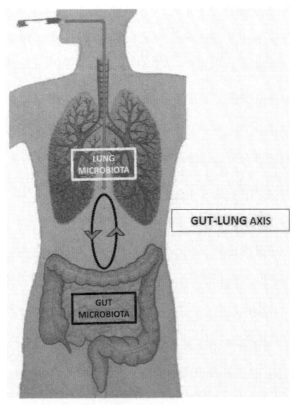

An understanding of the relationship between the lungs and large intestine is found in traditional oriental medicine, going back thousands of years

Further reinforcing this connection, researchers at the Francis Crick Institute discovered that disruptions in the intestinal microbiome resulting from antibiotics leave the lungs vulnerable to flu viruses and lead to more severe infections. As reported in *Science Daily*, in studies on mice, investigators found that signals from intestinal bacteria help to maintain a first line of defense in the lining of the lung. Eighty percent of mice with a healthy intestinal microbiome survived flu infection, while only one-third given antibiotics prior to infection survived.

"We found that antibiotics can wipe out early flu resistance, adding further evidence that they should not be taken or prescribed lightly," explains Dr. Andreas Wack, who led the research at the Francis Crick Institute. "Inappropriate use not only promotes antibiotic resistance and kills helpful gut bacteria, but may also leave us more vulnerable to viruses. "We were surprised to discover that the cells lining the lung, rather than immune cells, were responsible for early flu resistance induced by antibiotics," says Andreas. "Previous studies have focused on immune cells, but we found that the lining cells are more important for the crucial early stages of infection. They are the only place that the virus can multiply, so they are the key battleground in the fight against flu. Gut bacteria send a signal that keeps the cells lining the lung prepared, preventing the virus from multiplying so quickly.

A Google search on "diet, microbiome, and immunity" yielded many results. Research has shown that gut bacteria help develop immune cells, and also that immune cells help beneficial bacteria overcome the negative effects of harmful bacteria. High-fiber diets have been found to prevent microbes from eating away the lining of the colon, thus protecting against infection. Other studies have found that high animal food diets increase the risk of inflammatory bowel disease (IBD), while plant-based diets reduce risk and increase healthy diversity in the gut microbiota. Short chain fatty acids (SCFAs) are believed to improve colon health and lower the risk of inflammation. Researchers have found higher levels of SCFAs in subjects eating a plant-based diet, including a healthy Mediterranean diet. Plant-based diets high in fiber reduce intestinal transit time, or the time needed for food to travel through the digestive system. Protein breakdown was found to increase so-called "degradation" products in the colon. One of the researchers summarized the findings: "You can help food pass through the colon by eating a diet rich in fiber and drinking plenty of water. It may also be worth trying to limit for example meat, which slows down the transit time and provides the gut bacteria with lots of protein to digest." –*Science Daily*, June 27, 2016

Antibiotics and meat characterize the modern world. Both damage digestive health, the composition and function of the gut microbiome, and the body's immune response. Reliance on both extremes makes individuals more prone to serious infection by contagious viruses. The implications for the current pandemic are readily apparent, in terms of the origin of the virus, its mode of transmission, and the susceptibility of individuals to either serious, mild, or no infection. All indications point to the protective value of a plant-based diet, and the necessity of ending our dependence upon animals as a source of food. First, the mishandling of wild and exotic animals is suspected as the origin of the virus and its jump from animals to humans. Secondly, the risk of infection increases with the level of immune dysfunction. Risk goes up as immune function goes down, in direct proportion. Stronger immunity equals less risk of infection. The evidence implicating a high meat diet in disruption of the gut biome, and thus the body's immune function, is clear. A diet dependent upon animal foods weakens natural immunity while providing a breeding ground for virus infection. Once again, a lightfood diet strengthens natural immunity and counteracts infectious viruses spawned in darkness.

Like the flood of Deucalion, the flood of Manu, and the flood that destroyed the Aztecs' "Fourth Sun," the biblical deluge was the end of a world age. A new age succeeded it: our own, populated by the descendants of Noah. From the very beginning, however, it was understood that this age too would in due course come to a catastrophic end. As the old song puts it, "God gave Noah the rainbow sign; no more water, the fire next time."

GRAHAM HANCOCK

13

COMING OF AGE IN THE
AGE OF LIGHT

We have several milestones coming up in the twenty-first and early twenty-second century. The first is the year 2036. According to Michio Kushi, 2036 is the center of a spiral of human history that began millions of years ago, when our ancestors started to eat grain and walk upright, precipitating human brain development and the ability to see the entire universe. That spiral, most of it unrecorded, is now reaching the center and that will occur, according to Michio's prediction, in 2036. We refer to that center as "convergence." That date almost perfectly matches the year 2038 recorded in the timeline of the Great Pyramid as the time when human history comes to an end and, should universal destruction be avoided, a new history begins. (See *One Peaceful World*, by Michio Kushi, Square One Publishers, 2017.)

The second pivotal date is 2102. That date marks an important milestone in the great cycle above the North Pole. The Earth is like a spinning top or gyroscope. It spins on its axis and also wobbles. In the case of the Earth that motion is difficult for us to perceive as it moves slowly from our perspective. It takes about 25,000 years for the Earth to make a complete wobble; more precisely 25,800 years. Known in ancient times, the Greeks named this cycle the "Great Year." The Earth's axis is tilted about 23 degrees off from due north. If you extend a line from the earth's axis out into space, the twenty-five thousand year cycle caused by the wobbling motion describes a circle. Like our solar year, this cycle is divided into two opposite periods, one of darkness and the other of light, or one of night and the other day. The opposite poles of that cycle are two stars that appear over the North Pole, approximately 12,000 years apart. One is the star Vega in the constellation Lyra, and the other is the star Polaris in the small dipper, or small bear constellation, also known as Ursa Minor. This cycle has a profound effect on civilization and history. As the cycle proceeds, various stars and constellations appear over the North Pole and are gradually replaced by others. Our current North Star is the star Polaris.

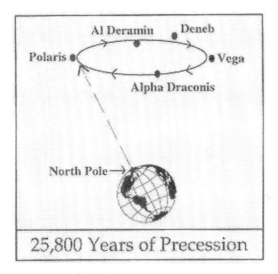

The cycle of the North Pole

Opposite to that, in 14,000 AD, 12,000 years from now, Vega will appear over the North Pole. Vega was also over the North Pole 12,000 years ago. Polaris will come most directly over the Pole in the year 2102. According to Wikipedia:

Due to the axial precession of the Earth, true north rotates in an arc with respect to the stars that takes approximately 25,000 years to complete. Around the year 2100 to 2102, Polaris will make its closest approach to the celestial North Pole.

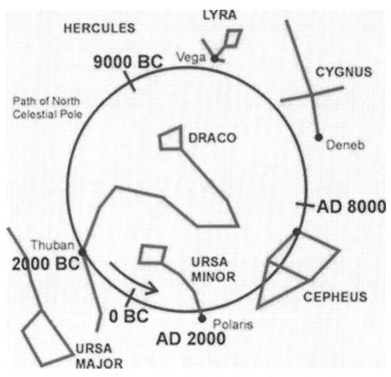

Precession of stars and constellations over the North Pole

If you look at astronomy charts, Google Sky, or the night sky with the naked eye, you see the next arm, or spiral band of the Milky Way galaxy, in which millions of stars are arranged in a belt that resembles a silver river. The Milky Way belt allows us to divide the 25,000-year cycle into a period of light and a period of darkness. Roughly 2,000 years from now, the North Pole will point directly into the belt of the Milky Way. The outer spiral arm of the galaxy serves to concentrate and amplify energy from the universe beyond. That will result in an influx of energy into the planet through the North Pole. This period is the period of brightness and energy—an age of light. We can also refer to it as the spring/summer or morning/day phase of the cycle. Opposite to that, when the pole points away from the galactic arm, is a period of darkness and diminished energy, something like the autumn/winter or evening/night phase of the cycle. It represents a 12,000-year age of relative darkness.

The Earth is a massive conductor of electric and magnetic energy. Energy from the periphery of the galaxy enters the planetary sphere at the North Pole. Energy from the center of the galaxy enters at the South Pole. Energy spirals down into the poles from outer space. Energy from both poles converges deep within the planet's interior and creates a highly magnetized core. The Earth's core spins at a different rate of speed than the crust, and is made of hot liquid iron. It generates a magnetic field that radiates out to the surface of the planet and beyond. These surface channels, which we can term Earth meridians, are the invisible force behind the formation of mountain ranges. These powerful currents of energy stream down from the peaks toward the valleys, continually dividing into smaller and smaller fractal streams. This is similar to the manner in which snowmelt streams down from the tops of mountains into the valleys below, forming rivers, streams, and other channels of fresh water. These invisible branches link the entire planet in an invisible energy grid. Any changes in the intensity of energy at the Poles will thus produce a corresponding change in the planet's energy system, with profound effects on plant, animal, and human life.

Before 12,000 years ago the Earth's North Pole pointed into the galactic arm. Worldwide mythology refers to that epoch as an age of paradise or a golden age. The Book of Genesis refers to that time as the Garden of Eden. Genesis also describes destruction by a great flood, as do other ancient myths and legends. Writing in his 1995 book, *Magicians of the Gods*, author Graham Hancock states, "An extinction level cataclysm occurred on our planet between 12,800 and 11,600 years ago. This event was global in its consequences and it affected mankind profoundly. In particular it must be considered as a reasonable hypothesis that worldwide myths of a golden age brought to an end by flood and fire are true, and that an entire episode of the human story was rubbed out in those 1,200 cataclysmic years between 12,800 and 11,600 years ago—an episode not of unsophisticated hunter-gatherers but of advanced civilization." Hancock goes on to state that the more than 2,000 flood myths from the ancient past all point to the same event. He further presents the megalithic structure at Gobekli Tepe in Turkey, believed to have been constructed 12,000 years ago, as an illustration of the sophistication of preflood civilization. He also references Plato's writings on the lost continent of Atlantis as corroboration. (Other investigators have backdated the construction of the Sphinx and Great Pyramid to that same period, possibly offering further proof of a highly developed pre-catastrophe civilization.)

More than 50 years ago, Michio Kushi proposed that the great flood was due to a polar shift that displaced continents and oceans, and that caused the melting of glaciers and the end of the Ice Age. He proposed that these shifts occurred periodically and lined up with the 25,800-year cycle of the pole star. The 25,800-year cycle itself has two opposite poles, each roughly 12,000 years apart. One of the poles is reached when the star Vega, in the constellation Lyra is overhead. The opposite pole occurs when Polaris, in the constellation Ursa Minor, or the Small Bear, appears over the North Pole. When Vega is overhead, as it was 12,000 years ago, global destruction occurs through the medium of water—the great flood. When Polaris is overhead, as it is at present, humanity faces destruction by the opposite medium—fire—in this case, through modern technology.

In part, Kushi's theory lines up with the theory known as Earth Crust Displacement. Developed by Harvard University's Charles Hapgood and published in the 1958 book, *Path of the Pole*, the theory states that polar wandering, or changes in the position of the Earth's poles, occurs because the outer shell of the planet shifts from time to time, moving some territories toward and others away from the poles, thus producing changes in their respective climates. (Graham Hancock likens the movement of the Earth's crust to "the loose skin of an orange moving around the fruit.") Hapgood writes in the introduction to his book, "This book will present evidence that the last shift in the earth's crust (the lithosphere) took place in recent time, at the close of the last ice age, and that it was the cause of the improvement in climate." Hapgood claimed that modern knowledge of geomagnetism, or the study of the polarization of rocks in the planet's crust by the Earth's magnetic field, led to the discovery that the Earth's poles "have changed their places on the surface of the earth at least 200 times since geological history began," and that the number of polar shifts could be "twice as long, or even longer." Hapgood further states:

I have found evidence of three different positions of the North Pole in recent time. During the last glaciation in North America the pole appears to have stood in Hudson Bay, approximately Latitude 60 degrees North and Longitude 89 degrees West. It seems to have shifted to its present site in the middle of the Artic Ocean in a gradual motion that began 18,000 or 17,000 years ago and was completed by about 12,000 years ago. The radioactive dating methods further suggest that the pole came to Hudson Bay about 50,000 years ago, having been located before that time in the Greenland Sea, approximate in Latitude 73 degrees North and Longitude 10 degrees East. Thirty thousand years earlier the pole may have been in the Yukon District of Canada.

If polar shifts align with the 25,000-year cycle, specifically with the placement of Vega over the North Pole, the most recent shift of 12,000 years ago matches that timeframe. The previous Vega as pole star epoch would have been 25,000 years earlier, or around 36,000 years ago. That may line up with Hapgood's estimate of the movement of the pole to Hudson Bay. His estimate of the pole being in the Yukon previous to that would approximate one Vega-cycle before that, with Vega being over the pole 60,000 years ago. These dates don't line up perfectly, but keep in mind that Hapgood's estimates are approximations, especially the further back in time he projects.

One problem with Hapgood's theory is the length of time it takes for the shift to occur. Hapgood stated that it took about 2,000 years for the North Pole to move from its previous position to its current location. In his 2015 book, *Magicians of the Gods*, Graham Hancock cites evidence that the shift happened much more rapidly. He proposes a newer hypothesis, which claims that the great flood was caused by impact with fragments of a comet that broke up above the Earth. The incoming fragments caused the Earth's poles to shift quite rapidly, bringing the Ice Age to a sudden end, causing global flooding and the extinction of many animal species. This is similar to the theory that the extinction of the dinosaurs was the result of a comet striking the earth 65 million years ago. However, linking such global catastrophes to such apparently random events doesn't account for the apparent cyclic or recurring nature of polar shifts. Regarding the dinosaurs,

Kushi proposed that their extinction was caused by a gradual cooling of the atmosphere in response to movement of the solar system around the galaxy, in a cycle he referred to as the "galactic year."

Regardless of the cause, myths and legends from around the world describe the previous world age ending in a catastrophic flood at the point in the North Pole cycle when the star Vega is directly overhead. Kushi postulated that when we arrive at the opposite pole 12,000 years after that, when Polaris appears over the pole, humanity faces destruction by fire. Water destruction is a natural event. Destruction by fire is manmade. According to Kushi, the last 12,000 years was a period of darkness and low energy resulting from the North Pole pointing away from the high energy belt of the Milky Way. To compensate for that reduction in natural energy, humanity turned to increasingly intense forms of artificial energy, in the form of technology, to make balance.

Five thousand years ago, low intensity forms of energy were in general use. Wood, charcoal, and biofuels were burned in the home for light and heat, and used as cooking fuel. It was not until the Industrial Revolution that civilization began to harness the power of steam in centralized factories. The 1800s saw coal, petroleum (oil), and electricity come into use. The twentieth century saw the spread of nuclear energy, the most concentrated, centralized, and highly intense among all previous forms of energy. The application of fire in the form of energy technology has become increasingly intense, centralized, and in use around the globe.

The development of artificial fertilizer marked a giant leap in this process. Nitrogen is used by plants to form amino acids and proteins, which are essential nutrients. For centuries, farmers obtained nitrogen by composting, adding manure from animals, or alternating their crops. Certain bean crops, called legumes, have root structures that enable bacteria, known as nitrogen-fixing bacteria, to pull in and "fix" nitrogen from the atmosphere, forming natural fertilizer, which the plants use. However, inherent in these processes are limits to the amount of food that is produced and, by extension, to the growth of human population. That changed in the early part of the 20th century when engineers developed an energy-intensive method to extract nitrogen from the atmosphere, literally from thin air. Nitrogen is about 80% of the atmosphere. However, it exists not as a single atom but as a molecule consisting of two atoms of nitrogen, or N_2. These atoms are not identical. They spin in opposite directions, and are strongly polarized. The nitrogen molecule is thus highly stable. Two German engineers, Fritz Haber and Carl Bosch developed a method to separate the atoms in the nitrogen molecule and produce ammonia, a nitrogen compound, which is then used to manufacture nitrate.

Nitrate is highly volatile and was used initially to manufacture explosives and munitions. It was the main force behind the explosive power of World War II. After World War II the focus shifted toward nitrogen-based fertilizer.

According to Wikipedia:

The Haber process now produces 450 million tons (440,000,000 long tons; 500,000,000 short tons) of nitrogen fertilizer per year, mostly in the form of anhydrous ammonia, ammonium nitrate, and urea, 3–5% of the world's natural gas production is consumed in the Haber process (~1–2% of the world's annual energy supply). In combination with pesticides, these fertilizers have quadrupled the productivity of agricultural land. Due to its dramatic impact on the human ability to grow food, the Haber process served as the "detonator of the population explosion," enabling the global population to increase from 1.6 billion in 1900 to today's 7 billion. Nearly 80% of the nitrogen found in human tissues originated from the Haber-Bosch process.

Using plant genetics, high yield varieties (HYV) of crops were developed to accept the newly available nitrogen fertilizer. The production of wheat, corn, and rice skyrocketed, and following that, world population exploded. Tampering with humanity's staple foods, especially the cereal grains, results in profound consequences. As a result, the human population went from 1.6 billion in 1900 to 7 billion today. Such an increase is an example of what is called exponential growth. At the beginning, an exponential curve increases slowly and incrementally, but as the increase continues, it reaches a tipping point at which growth dramatically skyrockets. The growth of the world's population has reached that stage.

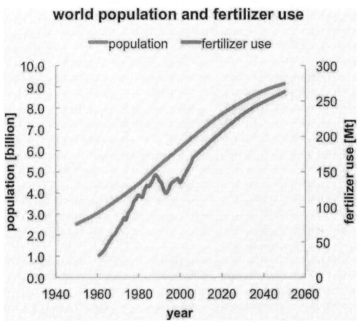

world population and fertilizer use

Increasing fertilizer use (lower line) prompted increases in world population (upper line) in the 20th and 21st century

Together with growth in population has been the concentration of the population into cities. Both of these trends are unsustainable. The United Nations estimates that half of the world's population is now living in cities, and that by 2050 about 64% of the developing world and 86% of the developed world will be living in urban centers. Much of this growth will occur in Asia and Africa. This concentration represents a dramatic shift from the past. Until the 18th century, the vast majority of the population lived in the countryside and engaged in farming and food production. Only 8% to 13% of the population of Europe lived in cities in 1800. That changed rapidly with the Industrial Revolution as the urban population skyrocketed due to continual migration from the countryside to the new industrial centers. Urbanization rapidly spread across the Western

World and by the mid-twentieth century, accelerated also in the developing world. In 1900, just 15% of the world population lived in urban areas. The United Nations reported that the percentage of people living in cities passed the 50% mark in 2007. The trend toward urbanization, shown in the graph below, represents the concentration of people in dense population centers, isolated from the countryside. It is part of the overall trend toward tightening or convergence as humanity approaches the center of the historical spiral.

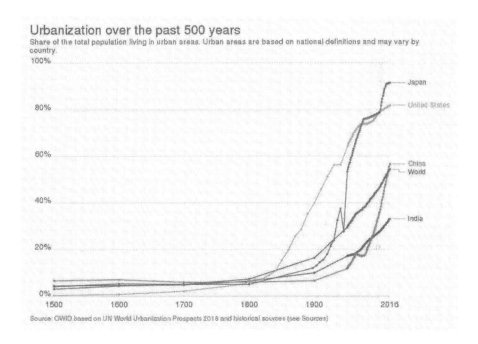

In the United States, high yield soybeans and corn are not used for direct consumption but fed to livestock. They are eaten indirectly in the form of beef, pork, and other animal products. Seventy percent of these crops are used to feed livestock. The modern diet is based on mass-produced, factory-farmed animal food. Food production is highly centralized. Millions of animals are confined in artificial spaces in a system known as "confinement agriculture." That system is inefficient and unsustainable. It takes thirteen pounds of grain to produce one pound of beef. It also takes 2,400 gallons of water to produce one pound of meat. These are not good returns. The modern food system is depleting the Earth's natural resources. The prevalence of meat and dairy in the modern diet has also led to the dramatic rise of degenerative illnesses like cancer and heart disease. Moreover, the animals themselves are sick and weak, contributing to an increasingly unhealthy food supply.

Humanity and planet Earth are headed for a collision. The clash will be between population growth on one hand, and limited water, energy, and natural resources on the other. The trend lines all point to negative exponential growth, including such trends as rain forest and ozone depletion, habitat destruction, the depletion of fish, pollution of the ocean, and the extinction of species. These trends are the result of the spread of modern technology, including the modern food system, around the globe, in combination with explosive growth in the human population. These trends, which are the hallmarks of the modern way of life, are clearly unsustainable.

Counterbalancing these tendencies is a growing trend toward local, organic, and sustainable farming and food production. Organic farmers don't use fertilizers and pesticides, but employ sustainable practices such as crop rotation, composting, the revival of heirloom seeds and crops. One example of that positive trend is that farmers in New England have started growing organic rice (see Appendix.) Several are producing it commercially. It was once thought that rice would not grow in the Northeastern U.S., due to the cold climate and short growing season. But apparently local farmers have succeeded. In the Pioneer Valley of Western Massachusetts, Christian Elwell, founder of South River Miso, has been growing rice for over thirty years, both on dry land and in a traditional rice paddy. Each step in the growing cycle is managed by hand, not by machine, including planting, harvest, threshing, hulling, and storage. Currently, a small group of farmers in Vermont, Massachusetts, New York, Maine, and New Jersey are planting and harvesting organic rice. Small-scale organic rice farming now has the potential to spread across the United States, transforming the landscape and culture, and diet and health of the American people.

Storing freshly harvested rice at South River Miso in Massachusetts

The trend toward organic farming is worldwide. In a Parliamentary Address, Russian President Vladimir Putin stated his desire to see Russia become the world's leading exporter of organic food. According to an article by Bryan MacDonald entitled, "Putin wants Russia to become world's organic superpower..." published online at rt.com:

Readers who have flown over Russia will have noticed the almost complete absence of intensive farming when compared with Europe or North America. The only real exception here is the southern Krasnodar region, which benefits from a very benign climate. There is little doubt that if Russian got its act together in this regard, it could probably feed the whole planet. In the 21st century, Russian food production has improved. Now, Putin is proposing a major focus on the area. "By 2020, Russia must provide itself with all food," he implored. "We need to cultivate the millions of acres now idle." The President suggested confiscating unused farmland and its sale to new owners willing to till it. As the Kremlin has rejected the idea of GMO food production, now a mainstay of American agriculture, Russia could become the world's principal supplier of high-quality organic food. Meaning there is potential to dominate the "high-end" market in both the West and in other wealthy countries—like China and the Middle Eastern states. "We are not only able to feed ourselves taking into account our lands, water resources–Russia is able to become the largest world supplier of healthy, ecologically clean and high-quality food which the Western producers have long lost, especially given the fact that demand for such products in the world market is steadily growing," said Putin.

In Russia, up to 50% of food is produced by small household gardens called dachas. Dachas produce 80% of the nation's fruit and berries and 66% of its vegetables. In colonial times, 90% of Americans earned their livelihood through farming. Today, farming and ranching employ only 1%. Highly centralized factory farms have put the family farm out of business. The United States and much of the world is completely dependent on industrial agriculture. The control of America's food supply is being concentrated into fewer and fewer hands. The supply lines are stretched thin and are highly vulnerable to disruption. A similar trend has occurred in retail merchandizing. In the past, businesses were locally owned. Small, mom and pop retailers, including clothing, hardware, and food stores have been put out of business by Wal-Mart and other nationwide chains. We see the same thing in the natural food industry. In the 1970s, most natural food stores were locally owned. Now the natural food industry has become increasingly centralized with the rise of big national chains. As the drawbacks of such increasing centralization become clear, society will shift back toward distributed agriculture, commerce, and industry, and increasingly toward local autonomy and control. That movement will develop hand in hand with a largescale shift from an animal- to a plant-based diet.

As we saw above, in 2102 the star Polaris will be over the North Pole. From that point onward, the Pole will begin a slow path that will eventually point it directly into the belt of the Milky Way. That era, which existed in the remote past, corresponded to the mythological golden age. According to Kushi, the influence of the Milky Way creates a supercharged soil, atmosphere, and food supply. In these conditions, human instinct and intuition are finely tuned with the universe. Higher consciousness prevails due to the direct channeling of galactic energies and human lifespan increases due to a superior quality of grains, vegetables, and other staple foods. Farming becomes less dependent upon human intervention, and more of a natural and organic process. The key to these developments is the ability to channel the energy of the Milky Way, both indirectly through the foods we eat and directly through the environment itself.

Rice and other cereals channel the energy of the universe directly through their awns, the antennae-like projections that extend from each grain. Eating whole grains on a daily basis makes that energy available and conditions the human brain to process it. As we have seen, meat and animal foods do not channel this energy. Not only does a diet based on animal food block reception of the universe, it also conveys the dark, limited, and miserable vibrations of the unfortunate creatures used for food. Animal foods cause calcification in and around the pineal gland, blocking its perception of the invisible spiritual universe. Complementing the internal influence of food are the combined influences of the Earth's environment, including those of the atmosphere and the nearby space surrounding the planet. Ideally, for maximum reception of universal energy, these zones are clear and unpolluted. Today, however, clear and direct reception of the universe, both for us and for cereal plants and other forms of vegetation, is being challenged by the following factors.

Air Pollution
Air pollution is a byproduct of industrialization and urbanization. The concentration of pollution in cities has led to increased incidence of respiratory diseases, including asthma. Not only are the gases, particulates, and biological molecules that pollute the atmosphere detrimental to health, they also block natural light and radiation from the night sky. Together with industry and transportation, diet is a major contributor to air pollution. Industrial meat production is a leading cause of greenhouse gas emissions and particulate matter pollution. Modern meat processing produces byproducts such as endotoxin, hydrogen sulfide, ammonia, and particulate matter such as dust. These are released together with methane and CO_2,

both greenhouse gases. The effects on health can be devastating. Meat and other animal foods are the leading cause of acidifying emissions that result in acid rain (see the chart below from Wikipedia.) Industrial hog farms release airborne animal particulates from confinement pens, manure collection pits, and disposal of waste. The modern meat industry creates a haze of death that offends not only the sense of smell but also blocks access to the spiritual vibrations of the universe. Note how peas and tofu, both plant foods, produce a fraction of the air pollution produced by beef, cheese, pork, and other animal foods.

Mean acidifying emissions **(air pollution) of different foods per 100g of protein**[19]	
Food Types	**Acidifying Emissions (g SO_2eq per 100g protein)**
Beef	343.6
Cheese	165.5
Pork	142.7
Lamb and Mutton	139.0
Farmed Crustaceans	133.1
Poultry	102.4
Farmed Fish	65.9
Eggs	53.7
Groundnuts	22.6
Peas	8.5
Tofu	6.7

Noise Pollution

Urbanization and industrialization have led to an epidemic of noise pollution. The harmful effects of traffic, airplanes, industry, construction, and lawn care, and other forms of artificial sound on humans and animals are becoming increasingly apparent. High noise levels contribute to stress and can result in cardiovascular disorders, high blood pressure, hearing loss, sleep disturbances, and cognitive decline. According to the European Environmental Agency, traffic noise levels above 55 decibels affect more than 100 million Europeans, the point at which noise becomes harmful to human health. Noise pollution also has harmful effects on wildlife, including those on land and in lakes, rivers, and the ocean. Noise pollution not only produces harmful physical effects, but also blocks the vibration and sound of nature, including the subtle, high frequency vibrations of the Milky Way. Artificial noise is impeding our perception of the subtle "music of the spheres" as well as the more immediate and soothing sounds of nature.

Space Debris

Space debris is defined as defunct manmade objects in space, mostly in orbit around Earth, which are no longer functional. It includes derelict spacecraft and fragmented debris from the breakup of rocket bodies and craft. The problem dates back to the first launch of satellites into Earth orbit in 1957. The U.S. Space Surveillance Network reports that as of October 2019, there were nearly 20,000 artificial objects in orbit above the Earth, including 2,218 functioning satellites. This figure is limited to objects large enough to be tracked. Smaller objects are far more numerous. According to Wikipedia:

- As of 2009, 19,000 debris over 5 cm (2 in) were tracked
- As of July 2013, estimates of more than 170 million debris smaller than 1 cm (0.4 in), about 670,000 debris 1-10 cm, and approximately 29,000 larger pieces of debris are in orbit
- As of October 2019, nearly 20,000 artificial objects in orbit above the Earth, including 2,218 operational satellites

In 2011, the U.S. National Research Council issued a report warning NASA that the problem had reached a critical point. According to Wikipedia: "According to some computer models, the amount of space debris 'has reached a tipping point, with enough currently in orbit to continually collide and create even more debris, raising the risk of spacecraft failures.' The report called for international regulations limiting debris and research of disposal methods." The problem is getting worse. In 2019, SpaceX, the private rocket company founded by Elon Musk, launched a pod of Starlink satellites, the first in a planned satellite constellation consisting of as many as 42,000 orbiters with the goal of providing internet access to all corners of the globe. In January 2021, a single SpaceX rocket boosted 140 satellites into Earth orbit. Other companies, including Amazon, are planning their own satellite networks. Estimates are that there could be as many as 50,000 soon encircling the planet.

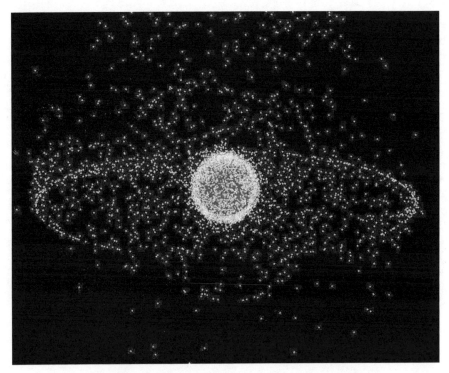

Computer model of the Earth surrounded by space debris

Due to outcry from astronomers, who pointed out that the satellites interfere with their view of the cosmos, SpaceX agreed to darken the satellites, tweak the orbits so they fly further from Earth, and change the orientation of their solar panels to reflect less sunlight back toward the ground. These changes may have eased the concern of the astronomers but they do not change the fact that an artificial metallic cloud is spreading around the Earth, beaming electromagnetic pollution toward the Earth, and scrambling, distorting, and blocking incoming light and energy from the galaxy and the night sky.

Electromagnetic Pollution

The Earth's atmosphere has seen a rapid proliferation of artificial electromagnetic fields in the last several decades. According to *The Lancet*, "The most notable is the blanket of radiofrequency electromagnetic radiation generated for wireless communication and surveillance technologies, as mounting scientific evidence suggests that prolonged exposure to radiofrequency electromagnetic radiation has serious biological and health effects." *The Lancet* goes on to explain:

> Due to the exponential increase in the use of wireless personal communication devices (e.g., mobile or cordless phones and WiFi or Bluetooth-enabled devices) and the infrastructure facilitating them, levels of exposure to radiofrequency electromagnetic radiation around the 1 GHz frequency band, which is mostly used for wireless communications, have increased from extremely low natural levels by about 10^{18} times. Radiofrequency electromagnetic radiation is also used for radar, security scanners, smart meters, and medical equipment (MRI, diathermy, and radiofrequency ablation.) It is plausibly the most rapidly increasing anthropogenic environmental exposure since the mid-20th century, and levels will surge considerably again, as technologies like the Internet of Things and 5G add millions more radiofrequency transmitters around us. Unprecedented human exposure to radiofrequency electromagnetic radiation from conception until death has been occurring in the past two decades. –Priyanka Bandara, David Carpenter, "Planetary electromagnetic pollution: it is time to assess its impact," *The Lancet*, Vol 2, December 2018.

Not only does electropollution have a negative impact on physical and mental health, it also affects our ability to receive energy from nature and the universe. The Earth and human beings resonate in the frequency, 7.8 Hz, as established by Alfred Schuman. Thus, humans are not affected by the planet's frequency. However, mobile phones, antennae of mobile towers, WiFi, cordless phones, tablets, and other wireless equipment work on much higher frequencies, ranging from 700 Megahertz (MHz) to 2.8 Gigahertz (GHz). The newer 5G networks are supposed to work on a frequency of 30 GHz to 300GHz. These high frequencies cause multiple resonances in the body's cells, leading to disturbances in communication between cells, including those of the brain and nervous system. The body's cells treat electromagnetic radiation as a stress factor, and react accordingly, and these reactions appear as ill health and disease. Electropollution also interferes with the ability of cereal grains to directly channel the universe's energy through their awns. According to *The Lancet*: "Evidence also exists of the effects of radiofrequency electromagnetic radiation on flora and fauna. For example, the reported global reduction in bees and other insects is plausibly linked to the increased radiofrequency electromagnetic radiation in the environment. Honeybees are among the species that use magnetoreception, which is sensitive to anthropogenic electromagnetic fields, for navigation." The awns in rice and other grains are sensitive and finely tuned to the vibration of the universe. The increase in electropollution threatens to disturb and block their reception of the vibrations of the night sky, including those of the Milky Way.

Light Pollution
In the *New World Atlas of Artificial Night Sky Brightness*, published in 2016, the authors map the global rise in artificial light pollution. The report is summarized in the Abstract:

Artificial lights raise night sky luminance, creating the most visible effect of light pollution—artificial skyglow. Despite the increasing interest among scientists in fields such as ecology, astronomy, health care, and land-use planning, light pollution lacks a current quantification of its magnitude on a global scale. To overcome this, we present the world atlas of artificial sky luminance, computed with our light pollution propagation software using new high-resolution satellite data and new precision sky brightness measurements. This atlas shows that more than 80% of the world and more than 99% of the U.S. and European populations live under light-polluted skies. The Milky Way is hidden from more than one-third of humanity, including 60% of Europeans and nearly 80% of North Americans. Moreover, 88% of Europe and almost half of the United States experiences light-polluted nights.

Suppression of melatonin is one of the many documented negative effects of light pollution. As we have seen, melatonin is secreted by the pineal gland and is essential for sleep. Reduction of melatonin disrupts sleep patterns and is associated with numerous long-term health risks. Light pollution is a leading disruptor of natural ecosystems, posing a serious threat to many nocturnal species, including flowers, birds, reptiles, bats, and amphibians. The effects of artificial night light on sea turtle hatchlings is especially concerning. Rather than being attracted by the safety of the ocean, many hatchlings are instead attracted away from the ocean by streetlights and other forms of artificial lighting and perish as a result. Skyglow and light pollution directly block the incoming light and energy of the night sky, including the Milky Way and other galaxies, diminishing our awareness of our universal origins.

Now, more than ever before, the clear light of the Milky Way, as well as the billions of stars in the visible universe, is being compromised. We could lose touch with our universal origins as well as with our future in the world of spirit. Whole grains, with their celestial channeling awns pointing toward the heavens, are receiving the energy of the night sky. In order to break through the metallic clutter, noise, and light deflection of today's atmosphere and night sky, and come into closer contact with the energy of the universe, it is vitally important to make whole grains the centerpiece of the human diet.

Today's scientists have substituted mathematics for experiments, and wander off through equation after equation as they build a structure that has no relation to reality.
NIKOLA TESLA

14

OUR PEACEFUL UNIVERSE

Recently I watched a BBC documentary titled, "The Big Bang." The show presented the big bang theory together with other explanations of how the universe came into being. The big bang represents one extreme of the spectrum of creation myths; in this case, the extreme end of the modern perspective. The person who came up with the big bang was a Belgian priest named Georges Lemaitre. His lifelong dream was to find a scientific theory that matched the biblical account of creation. His theory, known as the "big bang," stated that from nothing, from an infinitesimal point known as a "singularity," a giant explosion arose, throwing out all the matter in the universe. That explosion produced galaxies, stars, and planets; the entire known universe. Today, the prevalent view is that the universe is expanding. If the universe is expanding, that expansion had to have started somewhere, so believers in the big bang march that process backwards, and conclude that the universe must have originated as a single point in time and space. Their consensus is that the big bang took place about thirteen billion years ago.

Make no mistake. The big bang states that everything originated in a single violent act. Everything we see today, including all of us, had a violent origin. The big bang represents the epitome of scientific thinking. However, a major weakness in the big bang is its inability to provide an answer to the question, "What was there before the big bang?" The answer is often "nothing." The BBC documentary included creation stories proposed by theorists from India. Indian cosmologists believe that yes, the big bang occurred, creating the entire universe, but that there had to be something that existed prior to it. These cosmologists believe that what existed before the big bang derives from the Indian philosophy of karma, or never-ending cycles of cause and effect. The thinking goes something like this: "If the big bang produced expansion, it must have been preceded by cosmic contraction." Indian cosmologies posit that the big bang occurred, but that it followed the contraction of the previous universe. That contraction is known as the "big crunch." Once contraction reached a peak, the universe then began to expand. This is referred to as the "big bounce." My physicist friend, Dr. Mahadeva Srinivasan, was a proponent of this theory. However, questions as to how, why, and when these events occurred remain unanswered.

Most mainstream theories, as varied as they are, from East to West and back again, embrace the big bang. There is, however, a growing movement challenging the big bang's hegemony. Nevertheless, the big bang continues to dominate mainstream scientific thinking. Any research that attempts to go outside the big bang usually does not receive funding and is rejected for publication. The big bang has thus become a form of dogma that stifles free-thinking and objective research. In response, a group of scientists challenged the big bang in "An Open Letter to the Scientific Community," published in *New Scientist*, May 22, 2004. The contents of the letter are revealing.

The big bang today relies on a growing number of hypothetical entities, things that we have never observed—inflation, dark matter and dark energy are the most prominent examples. Without them, there would be a fatal contradiction between the observations made by astronomers and the predictions of the big bang theory. In no other field of physics would this continual recourse to new hypothetical objects be accepted as a way of bridging the gap between theory and observation. It would, at the least, raise serious questions about the validity of the underlying theory.

But the big bang theory can't survive without these fudge factors. Without the hypothetical inflation field, the big bang does not predict the smooth, isotropic cosmic background radiation that is observed, because there would be no way for parts of the universe that are now more than a few degrees away in the sky to come to the same temperature and thus emit the same amount of microwave radiation.

Without some kind of dark matter, unlike any that we have observed on Earth despite 20 years of experiments, big-bang theory makes contradictory predictions for the density of matter in the universe. Inflation requires a density 20 times larger than that implied by big bang nucleosynthesis, the theory's explanation of the origin of the light elements. And without dark energy, the theory predicts that the universe is only about 8 billion years old, which is billions of years younger than the age of many stars in our galaxy.

What is more, the big bang theory can boast of no quantitative predictions that have subsequently been validated by observation. The successes claimed by the theory's supporters consist of its ability to retrospectively fit observations with a steadily increasing array of adjustable parameters, just as the old Earth-centered cosmology of Ptolemy needed layer upon layer of epicycles.

Yet the big bang is not the only framework available for understanding the history of the universe. Plasma cosmology and the steady-state model both hypothesize an evolving universe without beginning or end. These and other alternative approaches can also explain the basic phenomena of the cosmos, including the abundances of light elements, the generation of large-scale structure, the cosmic background radiation, and how the redshift of far-away galaxies increases with distance. They have even predicted new phenomena that were subsequently observed, something the big bang has failed to do.

Supporters of the big bang theory may retort that these theories do not explain every cosmological observation. But that is scarcely surprising, as their development has been severely hampered by a complete lack of funding. Indeed, such questions and alternatives cannot even now be freely discussed and examined. An open exchange of ideas is lacking in most mainstream conferences. Whereas Richard Feynman could say that "science is the culture of doubt," in cosmology today doubt and dissent are not tolerated, and young scientists learn to remain silent if they have something negative to say about the standard big bang model. Those who doubt the big bang fear that saying so will cost them their funding.

Even observations are now interpreted through this biased filter, judged right or wrong depending on whether or not they support the big bang. So discordant data on red shifts, lithium and helium abundances, and galaxy distribution, among other topics, are ignored or ridiculed. This reflects a growing dogmatic mindset that is alien to the spirit of free scientific inquiry.

Today, virtually all financial and experimental resources in cosmology are devoted to big bang studies. Funding comes from only a few sources, and all the peer-review committees that control them are dominated by supporters of the big bang. As a result, the dominance of the big bang within the field has become self-sustaining, irrespective of the scientific validity of the theory.

Giving support only to projects within the big bang framework undermines a fundamental element of the scientific method—the constant testing of theory against observation. Such a restriction makes unbiased discussion and research impossible. To redress this, we urge those agencies that fund work in cosmology to set aside a significant fraction of their funding for investigations into alternative theories and observational contradictions of the big bang. To avoid bias, the peer review committee that allocates such funds could be composed of astronomers and physicists from outside the field of cosmology.

Allocating funding to investigations into the big bang's validity, and its alternatives, would allow the scientific process to determine our most accurate model of the history of the universe.

The big bang is not actually a theory, but a hypothesis. A hypothesis is a mental construct that must be tested and confirmed before it qualifies as a theory. There is no way to test or prove the big bang. As we see in the above critique, there is huge controversy within the scientific community due to the rigid adherence to the big bang and the refusal of mainstream science to investigate or fund alternate hypotheses.

Related to the big bang is another hypothesis which states that our sun is a huge thermonuclear reactor. In 1920, mathematician Arthur Eddington developed the idea that nuclear energy was being released in the sun's core. This idea gained credence following the creation of atomic weapons in the 1940s, a process that included the Manhattan Project, the explosion of atomic bombs over Hiroshima and Nagasaki, and the detonation of the first hydrogen bomb in 1950. According to David Talbott, "A new consensus arose, a conviction that only a fusion reactor at the sun's core could explain the sun's powerful emissions of heat and light. And now every student in the sciences reads about the hypothesis as fact." (*Discovering the Electric Sun*, Thunderbolts.info.)

Modern cosmologists believe the sun is a continually exploding hydrogen bomb in which, under great temperature and pressure, hydrogen is being transmuted into helium. (Hydrogen is the first element, helium the second.) The thermonuclear model is founded on Newton's idea of universal gravitation, in which the gravitational force of a star compresses its matter in on itself. As in a hydrogen bomb, tremendous centripetal or inward force produces great temperatures and pressures. These forces smash atoms into each other, causing them to fuse. This process releases tremendous energy, resulting in heat, light, charged particles, and radiation. In the gravitational model, the source of energy for the sun is the gravitational force of the sun itself. The sun is pulling mass toward its center. The sun will eventually exhaust its supply of nuclear fuel and burn out.

However, like the big bang, the concept of a thermonuclear sun is facing a serious challenge. A new scientific model threatens to replace it. The new model is based on studies of plasma and electricity as well as satellite observations such as those of Japan's Hinode spacecraft and NASAs fleet of Thermis spacecraft. It is also based on observations of the sun's corona, solar wind, sunspots, penumbra, and dramatic occurrences such as solar flares, prominences, and coronal mass ejections. At face value, the notion that all the stars in the universe, including our sun, are continually exploding hydrogen bombs is absurd. That would mean that all the light and energy of the universe exists due to the never-ending violence of nuclear fusion. The process in which cereal grains convert the light of the sun into glucose and the light from the stars into consciousness and spirit would thus be a byproduct of violent nuclear explosions. Clearly such a counterintuitive, nightmare vision is the product of a modern mind conditioned by over-reliance on animal foods that lead to a dark and deluded version of reality. The truth is far more sensible. The universe is a peaceful and orderly process in which the dimensions of reality, for example the world of pure energy, transition to the world of matter, including plant and animal life. Nuclear explosions are the product of the human mind, and not the natural evolution of the universe.

The new hypothesis, known as the "Electric Sun," states that the origin of the sun's energy is not the sun itself, but the electrically charged medium—the galaxy—that surrounds it. Thus, the sun is not a thermonuclear reactor powered by gravity, but a gigantic conductor of electricity. Critics of the thermonuclear sun point out that gravity is actually the weakest force in the universe—electrical energy is estimated to be 10^{39} power stronger than gravity. Nearly 70 years ago, Dr. C.E.R. Bruce, an astronomer and electric researcher, presented a new hypothesis about the sun. He suggested that the sun was an electrical discharge phenomenon: "It is not a coincidence that the photosphere has the appearance, the temperature and spectrum of an electric arc; it has arc characteristics because it is an electric arc, or a large number of arcs in parallel. These arcs quickly result in the neutralization of the accumulated space charge in their neighborhood and go out. They are not therefore stable discharges, but may rather be looked upon as transient sparks. Arcs thus continually appear and disappear. It is this coming and going which accounts for the observed granulation of the solar surface."

According to this hypothesis, most of the space in our galaxy contains plasma (electrically charged gas.) Plasma is made up of electrons, which have a negative charge, and ionized atoms, which have positive charge. Every charged particle in plasma has potential energy or voltage. The sun is the center of an immense plasma cell, called the heliosphere that stretches far out—several times the radius of Pluto—into space. The radius is estimated to be 18 billion km or 122 times the distance of the earth to the sun. The sun is positively charged in relation to the space around it. Negative electrons from space enter the sun from the outside while positive ions exit the sun, creating a plasma discharge like those seen in electric plasma laboratories. The sun is thus powered, not from within itself, but from the electric currents that flow from the galaxy in toward the sun. The sun's positive charge causes it to act as the anode in a plasma discharge. The negative charge, or cathode, originates far out in space at the edge of the heliosphere, in a region known as the *heliopause*, which as we saw above, is about 18 billion km from the sun. (For more on this, read *The Electric Universe*, by Wallace Thornhill and David Talbot, Mikimar Publishing, 2007.)

Keep in mind that the solar system is revolving around the center of the galaxy at enormous speed. The heliopause is located at the edge of this motion at the extreme periphery of the solar system. It generates high energy that complements and balances the electric charge of the central sun. The new model is consistent with our view that the energy powering the sun originates not from the sun itself, but from the periphery of the solar system and beyond into the galaxy itself. The sun is not a nuclear reactor, but the focus of a high-energy electric discharge.

Alternative views of the universe, for example that the big bang never happened and the electric sun, are closer to a peaceful natural cosmology than mainstream concepts like the big bang and thermonuclear sun. In the future, the big bang and similar notions based on a violent universe will be overturned. A new vision, more in line with the peaceful reality of existence, shall come to reign. That new vision could very well come from the cosmology of macrobiotics, a cosmology that links all phenomena in a grand unification. In macrobiotic cosmology, as defined by George Ohsawa and Michio Kushi, the universe is continually manifesting in the form of a logarithmic spiral originating in the infinite expansion. The oneness of infinity gives rise to space and time, beginning and end, front and back, and the countless sets of polarities that define our relative world. Polarization, which in macrobiotics we refer to as yin and yang, creates endless movement, energy, change, and evolution. In essence, the universe is comprised of energy, waves, or vibrations that eventually condense into matter. Spirals form in an inward or centripetal direction. Pure, diffuse energy becomes increasingly dense or contracted, creating subatomic particles such as electrons, protons, and neutrons; the world of atoms or elements; the vegetable world; and finally, the world of animals and human beings. The process of creation occurs in a spiral with seven stages.

1. One infinity (the eternally non-manifest or non-being; the source of all manifestation and all being.)
2. Polarization (the two primary forces—yin and yang—that give rise to being or manifestation.)

3. Energy (the first appearance of being; endless movement in the form of contracting and expanding spirals, fractal filaments and currents, etc.

4. Preatomic particles (condensed spirals of energy that take the form of electrons, protons, etc. It is here that the giant plasma currents appear that give rise to superclusters, local groups of galaxies, and individual galaxies.)

5. Elements (further condensed and complex spirals of energy that take the form of stars, planets, comets, interstellar gas, etc.)

6. Plant life (further complex fractal spirals of energy with self-replicating abilities.)

7. Animal life, and ultimately human beings.

The human form and consciousness is the most condensed, complex, and free of all energy spirals found in the universe, with multiple interacting fractal structures, both visible and invisible. The fractals found in human physiology are internal and hidden; those appearing in the plant world are the opposite—external, exposed, and apparent. They complement each other perfectly.

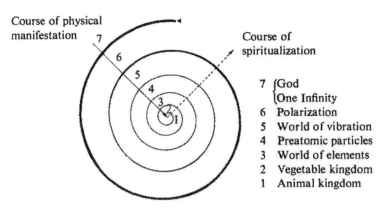

Spiral of materialization developed by Ohsawa and Kushi

In the macrobiotic view, the universe was not created at a fixed point in time, but is continually manifesting through what Ohsawa and Kushi named the "Spiral of Creation or Materialization." The universe is at all times new. Galaxies, stars, and planets, appear, exist for a while, and then vanish in cosmic cycles governed by universal law. New galaxies, stars, and planets then appear and follow the same universal law. The universal law of change—yin changes into yang; and yang changes into yin—exists beyond time and space. The process of creation is going on throughout the universe at this very moment. The process has no beginning and no end. Ohsawa understood that spirals form at the periphery, or outside, and wind inward toward the center. Here, they reverse course and begin an outward journey back toward the periphery. Galaxies exhibit this pattern, as does our solar system. Ohsawa, and later Michio Kushi, pointed out that the Sun's energy did not originate within the sun itself, but from the periphery of the spiral at which the sun is the center.

Proponents of the Electric Sun identify this spiral as the heliopause and agree that the energy that powers the sun originates at the periphery and not at the center. They suggest that the energy powering the sun is electrical and not gravitational or nuclear. In macrobiotic cosmology, the solar system, galaxy, and universe itself are created from the outside in, and not from the inside out, as suggested by the big bang and gravitational (nuclear) sun models. Even if we agree that electricity and magnetism, and not gravity, is the prime force of the universe, we need to progress beyond that to the origin of electricity and magnetism, which is the primary polarization of the universe. And progressing beyond that, we arrive at the infinite oneness of life itself, beyond time and space, beyond the relative changing universe, yet forever giving rise to the relative changing universe. In order to realize a peaceful world, we must see the universe, as it is, an endlessly manifesting, orderly and peaceful reality.

15

COOKING FOR INSTINCT, INTUITION, & NATURAL IMMUNITY

Because of their awns brown rice and other whole grains channel energy from the universe. Awned grains are ideal for activating the uppermost chakras where our intuition is centered. The origin of intuition is the universe. Our ability to channel and interpret the universe's signals determines the accuracy and depth of our intuitive faculties. At the same time, whole grains also benefit the chakras in the lower body. Grains are rich in fiber. The undigested fiber in whole grains serves as a prebiotic nutrient. It ferments in the colon and serves as nourishment for the microbiome, or colonies of beneficial bacteria that inhabit the digestive tract. Eighty percent of the body's immune cells are also located in the digestive tract. Thus, a healthy microbiome in turn strengthens our natural immunity.

When we cook brown rice (and other whole grains,) we are utilizing the most basic elements that make life possible. The first life element is the rice itself. Brown rice strengthens the pineal gland, the focus of spiritual vision and insight. In a temperate or four-season climate, we suggest using short grain brown rice as the primary grain. Select varieties that are organically grown. Other organic rice—such as medium and long grain varieties—can be used for enjoyment or to adapt to other climate conditions. Water is the next essential life element. Water quality has become a problem in the modern world. Municipal water is chemically treated and fluoridated and is not suitable for daily cooking. We recommend using natural spring or well water. Filtered water can be used if natural spring or well water is not available.

Salt is the next essential life element. Try to locate high quality natural sea salt. Grey salt is not recommended as it has too high a content of magnesium. After experimenting with a variety of natural sea salts, we selected Si Salt—processed from the clean Pacific waters off Baja, California—as ideal for daily use. Keep in mind that when adding salt to your brown rice, only a small pinch is needed. The fourth essential element is fire. As with water, the quality of fire is also problematic in the modern world. Cooking with fire has been replaced with artificial electric ranges and microwave ovens, both of which impart unnatural and potentially harmful radiation and both of which take away the delicate control necessary for healthful cooking. For this reason, we recommend cooking over a gas flame. As we saw in Chapter 7, most gourmet chefs reject electric cooking in favor of gas cooking. Our ancestors were in contact with fire on a daily basis. Fire is essential not only in cooking but also for warmth and shelter. We are the only species that has tamed fire (both for creative and for destructive purposes.) Taming fire was the first step in gaining mastery over our natural environment. (Those who are unable to access gas cooking in their kitchens are advised to purchase portable gas stoves and use these in the daily cooking of brown rice and other whole grains as well as soup and stock.)

Strive to make perfect brown rice on a regular basis. The rest of your cooking will come together in a grand symphony of natural harmony. There are many excellent cookbooks that describe how to prepare grains such as millet and barley, and how to incorporate whole grains into a varied and balanced plant-based diet. I especially recommend *The Changing Seasons Macrobiotic Cookbook* by Aveline Kushi and Wendy Esko (Avery, 2003) to help you get started.

Basic Brown Rice

1. Wash one cup of organic brown rice by covering with water, rinsing, and draining the water. Repeat three times.
2. Place in a pot with a tight-fitting lid. Add a small pinch of sea salt (optional) and 1 ½ – 2 cups of spring water.

3. Cover and bring to a boil on a medium high flame. When the rice comes to an active boil, reduce the flame to low and cook for 50-60 minutes.
4. Turn off the flame and let the rice sit for several minutes.
5. Remove from the pot with a wooden spoon and place in a serving bowl.

Brown rice may also be cooked in a pressure cooker. Bring 1 cup of washed grain to a boil in 1 ½ cups water and when pressure is up, place a flame deflector under the pot. Lower the flame and cook for 50 minutes. Brown rice and other whole grains can also be soaked prior to cooking, anywhere from one to several hours or even overnight depending upon one's condition and needs.

Soup and stock are especially beneficial for the small intestine chakra, the center of our instinct located opposite to the intuitive chakras. Why do soup and stock play such an important role? Why are they also considered essential for good health? There are a number of important reasons. The first is that soup prepares the digestion. That is why it is normally served at the beginning of the meal. Because it is primarily liquid, with ingredients that tend to be softer than usual, soup is easy to digest. As we all know, soup is often the first food served to someone who is ill. These beneficial effects are augmented by the fact that soups are seasoned with naturally fermented products such as miso (organic soybean paste) and shoyu (organic soy sauce.) These foods contain natural probiotics, including A. oryzae, that aid both in digestion and absorption, and supplement the stock of beneficial bacteria in the colon. The combination of naturally fermented seasonings, which are rich in probiotics, plus the sea vegetables used often in stock, activates the second, or small intestine chakra.

Another reason soup is important is that it can regulate our body temperature. This is especially important in cold weather. It is sometimes hard to guarantee that the various dishes in a meal will remain hot after serving. However, we can usually guarantee that soup will be hot. Hot soup improves circulation and warms the body. Warmth is important for maximum functioning of the small intestine chakra. Hot soup can restore vitality depleted by cold, damp weather. Hot tea also serves this purpose, but without the nutrients found in soup. Soup has a slightly salty taste that is achieved by adding seasonings such as sea salt, shoyu, or miso. These seasonings help the body, and especially the bloodstream, maintain a healthy alkaline condition. Simply put, soup builds strong blood. Since immunity is carried by specialized whiter blood cells, healthy blood is the origin of a healthy body and strong immunity.

Healthy, nourishing, and delicious soups begin with a simple stock. The ingredients for stock include wakame sea-vegetable (kombu can be substituted on occasion) and dried shiitake mushroom. These ingredients are the foundation of soup and broth. To prepare basic stock, place dried shiitake mushroom (one mushroom per cup of water) and wakame (a one- or two-inch piece per cup) in cold water. Bring to a boil, cover, and simmer until the wakame and shiitake are soft, tender, and easy to chew. As an alternate method, soak the shiitake and wakame separately for about 1-½ hours. Slice the wakame into bite-sized strips and do the same for the shiitake. You can remove the hard stem of the shiitake and the tough spine of the wakame for ease in chewing. Add the wakame and shiitake, plus the soaking water, to cold water. (Chopped vegetables can also be added at this time.) Cook as above. An experienced chef knows by taste, aroma, and color when the vegetable stock is done and ready for seasoning. This ability can only be gained through experience. I recommend that you taste your stock after about 10 to 15 minutes of simmering. Don't forget, basic vegetable stock made with dried shiitake mushroom and wakame is the foundation for healthy and nourishing soup.

Unseasoned stock has a clean, pure taste with a subtle hint of the ingredients used in the broth. It should not be too strong, but fresh and light. It should have a light, delicate, almost clear color. If the stock needs more cooking, meaning that the vegetables have not yet become tender, let it cook longer but sample it every five minutes or so to prevent overcooking. Once your stock has achieved perfection, it is time to add seasoning. You have one of two options. You can opt for a clear broth or a more full-bodied stock. The seasoning of choice for clear broth is high quality organic shoyu.

Illustration by Naomi Ichikawa Esko

Shoyu is a rich dark liquid. It adds a wonderful, slightly salty taste that blends perfectly with ingredients like wakame and shiitake. Since stock or broth is essential for health, use the highest quality natural and organic brands. Most high-quality brands are handcrafted in small batches, using techniques passed down from generation to generation. They use only the purest natural and organic ingredients. The secret to good shoyu broth is to add a small amount at the beginning, less than you think you need. I call this "under-adding." You can pour directly from the bottle into the broth. After each pour, ladle or spoon some broth into a bowl for sampling. If it is fine, leave it as is. If it requires more, add more. Repeat until the broth is perfect. Remember, you can always add more seasoning, but if you over-add, you can't take away what you've added. Properly seasoned clear broth has a light, translucent amber color and a slightly salty taste. You should be able to detect hints of the wakame and shitake. The saltiness of the shoyu should not overwhelm these subtle, delicate flavors.

Adding miso creates a more full-bodied stock. Unlike shoyu, which is a liquid, miso is a thick paste. The three main varieties of miso are mugi miso, made with fermented barley and soybeans, genmai miso, made with fermented brown rice and soybeans, and hatcho miso, made only with fermented soybeans. As with organic shoyu, we recommend using high quality natural and organic miso. Aside from these traditional varieties of miso, most of which are imported from Japan, you can also enjoy specialty miso, such as that made by South River Miso in Massachusetts and Miso Master in North Carolina. For example, our friends at South River invented several new types of miso such as dandelion-leek, chickpea, azuki bean, and garlic-red pepper miso.

The first key point in making miso soup is to properly dilute the miso paste before adding it to the broth. We do this by placing miso paste in a bowl (usually one teaspoon per cup of liquid), spooning broth from the soup pot over the miso, and mixing until the paste is completely dissolved. Dissolving the miso allows it to spread smoothly and evenly throughout the broth without forming clumps. Our goal is to achieve a consistently smooth broth. The second key point is the same as that for clear broth. "Under-add" at first. Taste a sample. If the taste is perfect, leave as is. If a stronger flavor is needed, add a little more until perfect flavor is achieved. Properly seasoned miso soup occupies that rare "sweet spot" in between bland and overly salty. Continual practice will help you identify and occupy that magical zone. Good miso soup is deep, rich, and satisfying.

Try not to use too many ingredients in your soups and other dishes until you understand the energetic nature of each ingredient and the positive or negative effect of combing it with the other ingredients in the dish. In and of itself, there is nothing wrong with variety. I'm in favor of diversity. Nature itself is nothing if not endlessly diverse and varied. However, in the quest for variety, be careful not to obscure the simple yet profound harmony that underlies all healthful cooking. "Keep it simple" is a good motto to keep in mind when cooking daily meals.

When learning to prepare soup and stock, I suggest that you first master the basic stock presented above, seasoning with shoyu for clear broth and miso for a more full-bodied soup. Once these basics have been mastered, we can enlarge the range of ingredients to include vegetables, whole grains, noodles, tofu, and others. Although they share many characteristics, clear shoyu broth and full-bodied miso soup are somewhat opposite. Shoyu is clear; miso is thick and full-bodied. Clear shoyu stock lends itself perfectly as a broth for things such as cooked noodles or leftover brown rice. Fewer vegetables are added so as to make room for these hearty ingredients. Miso, on the other hand, lends itself less to hearty noodles and brown rice and more to a variety of vegetables.

Noodles in broth are the perfect way to use shoyu broth. They serve as a one-dish meal. They are fun, nourishing, and satisfying. In cold weather, they are warming and vitality restoring. I can't imagine life without noodles in broth. To prepare, boil organic noodles such as udon, soba, somen, or other varieties until they are ready to eat. Rinse under cold water. Place in individual serving bowls and ladle hot broth over them to cover. Garnish with fresh chopped scallion or chive and enjoy. Once you master basic noodles in broth, you can add a variety of delicious, nourishing, and healthful toppings. Try adding things such as fried tofu, quick steamed greens, fried tempeh, and for special occasions, battered and deep-fried vegetables known as tempura. Once again, you can use noodles in broth as a quick, one dish meal. After you add selected toppings, don't forget to garnish appropriately.

As we have seen, miso soup has a thicker, more full-bodied texture. Vegetables tend to complement miso broth, although grains and noodles can be added on occasion. Common vegetables and combinations include:

> Daikon, wakame, shiitatke
> Carrot, onion, wakame, shiitake
> Kabocha (sweet fall squash), wakame, shiitake

Of course, there are many other combinations of vegetables, including leafy greens that contribute to nourishing miso soup. Root and round-shaped vegetables can be added to the cold water at the beginning, together with wakame and shiitake. Greens require less cooking and are best added at the end. Once again, we can't overemphasize the importance of strong nourishing stock and broth for overall health and wellbeing. Below is a summary of how to prepare basic miso soup and shoyu broth.

Miso Soup

1. Soak wakame (one-quarter to one-half inch piece per person) for about five minutes and cut into small pieces.
2. Soak dried shiitake mushroom (one mushroom per cup of liquid) for about five minutes and cut into small pieces, removing the hard stem.
3. Add the wakame and shiitake to fresh, cold water and bring to a boil. Meanwhile, cut some vegetables into small pieces. Add to the wakame and shiitake stock. Recommendations include: daikon; carrot and onion; sweet winter squash; and other fresh, local, and organic vegetables.
4. Add the vegetables to the boiling broth and boil for three to five minutes until the vegetables are soft and tender.
5. Dilute miso (one-half to one level teaspoon per cup of broth) in a little water, add to soup, and simmer for three to four minutes on a low flame.
6. Garnish each bowl or serving with fresh chopped scallion, chive, or parsley.

Simmer the soup for three to four minutes after you add miso to the broth. Don't bring the soup to a boil once the miso has been added. The broth should not have a harsh salty taste. From time to time include leafy greens (kale, collards, watercress, turnip or daikon greens.) Add them toward the end of cooking. You may occasionally use leftover grain or noodles to make a thicker soup. Cubed tofu may be added to the broth on occasion, usually toward the end of cooking.

Shoyu Broth
As with miso, it is essential to use high-quality organic shoyu (traditional soy sauce.) Like miso, shoyu is an essential ingredient in strengthening digestion, maintaining healthy blood, and fortifying natural immunity. Miso soup and shoyu broth strengthen the lower small intestine chakra and enhance its function in sharpening our instincts. (Note that those with gluten sensitivity may use organic gluten free tamari or other soy sauce.)

1. Soak wakame (one-quarter to one-half inch piece per person) for about five minutes and cut into small pieces.
2. Soak dried shiitake mushroom (one mushroom per cup of liquid) for about five minutes and cut into small pieces, removing the hard stem.
3. Add the wakame and shiitake to fresh, cold water and bring to a boil.
4. Reduce the flame to medium-low and simmer until the wakame and shiitake are tender.
5. Add organic shoyu to taste. The broth should not have a harsh salty taste. It is better to start with a small amount and add more if necessary. Simmer for several minutes. Turn off the flame and serve.

Ladle the broth over cooked udon, soba, or somen for hot noodles in broth. Ladle over leftover brown rice for hot rice soup, or drink as is for a hot alkalizing broth. Vegetables such as daikon, onion, carrot, or leafy greens may be added to the basic wakame/shiitake stock. Shoyu broth should be garnished with fresh chopped scallion, chive, or parsley.

If we were to go ahead and serve soup broth as is, without any further steps, quite frankly, our dish would not be balanced. Balance is achieved by utilizing counterpoint in our dishes. In the case of soup or broth, balance is achieved through garnish. Miso and shoyu are both fermented foods. Fermentation is a process of decomposition and breakdown, or in other words, expansion. However, miso and shoyu are salted and aged and these factors cause these foods to have an overall contractive effect. Dried wakame is a product of the salty ocean, and although it is one of the lighter sea vegetables, it is on the whole contractive due to its mineral content and the drying process. Shiitake are generally more expansive, as are mushrooms as a category. However, sun drying makes them concentrated. (Fresh shiitake are expansive; softer and juicier.) And, on the whole, the soup is cooked over fire, which, of itself, produces contraction. The ingredients are boiled and then simmered until tender.

Light, fresh, and upward energy help balance these contractive effects. Fresh chopped scallion provides a perfect energetic balance. (Chive or other finely chopped greens have a similar effect.) Scallion has a relatively small root but large stem and leaves. Most of its growth takes place above ground in an upward direction. It is green in color (green is cooler and more expansive than orange, brown, or red), and is used raw, which is crisper and more watery than cooked. So, on the whole, the upward energy of raw scallion balances the concentrated energy of cooked soup; the green color balances the brown or amber color of the broth; and the fresh raw energy of the scallion balances the dried and cooked energy of the wakame and shiitake in addition to the contractive energy of the aged miso. The overall effect of adding garnish is to catalyze, liberate, and activate the energy of the cooked broth, making it not only delicious and visually appealing, but also highly effective as a health-supporting and healing food.

There's something special about getting others involved during
the wedding ceremony—we throw bouquets, ask our friends and family
to be a part of our wedding parties, and eat and drink alongside loved
ones to create memories that last a lifetime. Tossing rice is a wedding
tradition that gets everyone involved, which may be why it's persisted
throughout the centuries. Exit tosses date back to the ancient Romans, but
how did the ritual start? In olden times, marriage meant expansion, from
building a family to increasing one's assets. Rice (most likely chosen for
its availability and low cost) symbolized both fertility and prosperity, and
tossing it at couples implied best wishes and good luck-for newborns,
good harvests, and everything in between.
Alternatives included wheat (the Roman tradition) and oats, but
regardless, the message was clear: Seeds and crops are things that grow.
EMILY PLATT

The true fertility foods are whole grains, healthy fats, excellent
protein packages…
THE FERTILITY DIET

AFTERWORD

Seeds of the Future

As we saw in Chapter 13, tampering with humanity's staple foods—the cereal grains—so as to produce high-yield varieties, led to exponential growth in the world's population as a whole. Such uncontrolled population growth, coupled with the global spread of a high-meat diet, threatens to deplete the Earth's resources while causing irreparable harm to the planetary ecosystem upon which life depends. Paradoxically, however, while population growth continues unabated in certain parts of the world, the developed economies of America, Europe, and Asia are facing a demographic crisis. Writing in her 2020 book, *Count Down: How Our Modern World is Threatening Sperm Counts, Altering Male and Female Reproductive Development, and Imperiling the Future of the Human Race* (Scribner), Shanna H. Swan, PhD. presented the situation as follows:

> It would require a couple to have an average of 2.1 babies to sustain a county's population through new births alone. But in most Western and in some Eastern countries, that benchmark isn't being achieved. In the United States, for example, the fertility rate, which is defined as the average number of children born per woman, was 1.8 in 2017, a 50 percent drop from 1960, according to data from the World Bank. In 2018, the United States had the lowest number of births in thirty-two years! In Italy and Spain, the fertility rate is now down to 1.3. In Hong Kong it has plummeted from 5.0 in 1960 to 1.1 in 2017, while in South Korea it has dropped from 6.1 in 1960 to 1.1 in 2017. And the number of babies being born in China fell to its lowest point since 1961, triggering what's being called a "looming demographic crisis."

Although there are many reasons for these declines, including couples postponing having children and a declining interest in sex among young adults, Dr. Swan points to a key biological metric: the catastrophic decline in male sperm counts and testosterone levels. Dr Swan was the lead author of the 2017 paper, "Temporal Trends in Sperm Count: A Systematic Review and Meta-Regression Analysis" that brought the world's attention to the modern sperm crisis. As she states in her book:

> It's not only that sperm counts have plummeted by 50 percent in the last forty years; it's also that this alarming rate of decline could mean the human race will be unable to reproduce itself if the trend continues. As my study collaborator Hagai Levine, MD, asks, "What will happen in the future— will sperm count reach zero? Is there a chance that this decline would lead to extinction of the human species? Given the extinction of multiple species, often associated with man-made environmental disruption, this is certainly possible. Even if there is low probability for such a scenario, given the horrific implications, we have to do our best to prevent it."

(c) St. van Appeldorn

Barley with awns

The crisis in fertility is most prevalent in richer countries with the highest meat consumption and the lowest consumption of whole grains, including New Zealand, Australia, Europe, and North America. It is also widespread in Asian countries where white rice has replaced the traditional brown rice in the diet, and where the Western diet has replaced traditional eating habits. Singapore, Macau, Taiwan, Hong Kong, and South Korea are all in the top ten countries with the lowest fertility rates. The decline in fertility is most likely the result of these dietary changes in combination with the increasingly widespread use of endocrine-disrupting chemicals, especially in plastics, in modern society. As Dr. Swan states:

> In particular, the ubiquity of insidiously harmful chemicals in the modern world is threatening the reproductive development and functionality of both humans and other species. The worst offenders: chemicals that interfere with our body's natural hormones. These endocrine-disrupting chemicals (EDCs) are playing havoc with the building blocks of sexual and reproductive development. They're everywhere in our modern world—and they're inside our bodies, which is problematic on many levels.

A lightfood diet based on organic whole grains, beans, vegetables and other plant foods holds the solution to problems with human fertility. In the case of overpopulation caused by the overuse of fertilizer and high-yield grains, a return to locally-based organic farming and a phasing out of chemically intensive industrial farming will help stabilize population growth. The population will begin to match the local natural resources available in each region. In the opposite case, where populations are facing serious decline, adoption of a plant-based diet centered on whole cereal grains will help boost natural fertility, especially if coupled with a phase-out of endocrine disrupting chemicals. The "Fertility Diet Study," published in 2007 by researchers at Harvard, found that women who ate less animal protein and more vegetable protein; more high-fiber, low glycemic carbohydrate-rich foods, including whole grains; and more vegetarian sources of iron and fewer meat sources had a 66% lower risk of ovulatory infertility and a 27%

reduced risk of infertility from other causes than women who didn't follow these dietary guidelines.

If we look closely at grains growing in the field, their relationship to human fertility becomes apparent. The awns channel energy from the cosmos. That energy converges with the cereal plant that extends upward from the Earth. Like the union of male and female, Heaven and Earth converge in each grain. Heaven's genetic inheritance fuses with that of the Earth to form the seed of new life, so as to continue the species into the endless future.

APPENDICES

Lightfood Principles

The first principle of lightfood eating is to select our foods in an ecological, environmentally conscious manner. That means to rely primarily on foods native to the climate and environment in which we live. Until the modern age, people were more or less dependent on the products of their regional agriculture. Foods that grew in their area formed the basis of their daily diet. It was not until modern technology that it became possible for people to base their diets on foods from regions with far different climates.

Today, it is common for people to consume bananas from South America, sugar from the Caribbean, pineapples from the South Pacific, or kiwi from New Zealand. However, our health depends on our ability to adapt to the changes in our environment. When we eat foods from a climate that is very different from ours, we lose that adaptability. As society moved away from its traditional, ecologically based diet, there has been a corresponding rise in chronic illness. Therefore, for optimal health, we need to return to a way of eating based on foods produced in our local environment, or at least on foods grown in a climate that is similar to ours.

Foods that are drier, harder, and more concentrated remain viable longer and can come from a greater distance than foods with a fragile, perishable, or expansive nature. Viable foods include sea salt and sea vegetables. Sea salt is a crystalized mineral. Dried sea vegetables are also rich in minerals. Foods such as these can come from the oceans around the world, provided these waters are within our hemisphere. Cereal grains, especially with the outer husk attached, remain intact for a long time, even thousands of years, and can come from anywhere in your continent. Dried beans also travel well and can come from a similarly wide area. However, vegetables and fruits are more delicate, perishable, and expansive; they decompose rapidly, and unless they are naturally dried or pickled, are best taken from our immediate area.

A second principle is to adapt our cooking and eating to seasonal changes. The modern way of eating does not do this, as people eat pretty much the same diet throughout the year. High temperatures and bright sunshine produce a stronger charge of upward energy in the environment. Water evaporates more rapidly and plants become lush and expanded. Spring and summer are times of upward, expansive energy. Then toward the end of summer, energy starts to change, moving downward and inward. In colder and darker conditions, such as those of autumn and winter, downward or contracting energy is stronger.

During spring and summer, we make our diet lighter and fresher, meaning that we use less fire in cooking. We do not need as much fire in our cooking because fire is already there in the form of strong sunshine. When it is hot, we do not need warmth from our food. As we move into autumn and winter, with cooler temperatures and stronger downward energy, we make our food hearty and warming by using more fire in cooking. As the seasons change, we also need to utilize the natural products of our environment. Our gardens are filled with vegetables and other foods during the spring and summer, so we can naturally eat plenty of fresh garden produce during these times. For example, summer is the time when corn is readily available, so it is fine to eat plenty of fresh corn in that season.

A third principle is to eat according to our distinctive human needs. As we saw in Chapter 2, our teeth reveal the ideal proportion of foods in the human diet. We have thirty-two adult teeth. There are twenty molars and premolars. The word *molar* is a Latin word for *millstone*, or the stones used to crush wheat and other grains into flour. These teeth are not suited for animal food, but for crushing or grinding grains, beans, seeds, and other tough plant fibers. There are also eight front incisors (from the Latin, *to cut*) and these are well suited for cutting vegetables. We also have four canine teeth. The canines can be used for animal food, not necessarily meat, but foods such as white-meat fish. The ideal proportion of foods as reflected in the teeth is five parts grain and other tough fibrous foods, two parts vegetables, and one-part animal food. The ideal ratio between plant and animal food is seven to one.

The modern diet does not reflect this pattern. Rather than whole grains, meat or other types of animal food are the primary foods. Vegetables are often used as garnish to the main course of animal food. Cereal grains are eaten almost as an afterthought, and are eaten in the form of white bread, white rolls, and other highly refined products. Refined bread or rolls are used simply as a vehicle to carry a hot dog, hamburger, or some other type of animal food. Grains are an incidental part of the modern diet. Today, the majority of people are eating the opposite of what they should be eating. That is why so many health problems exist in the modern world. However, that view is changing. The vanguard of modern nutrition now agrees that plant-based diets are better for our health. If we compare the health patterns of people who are eating plant-based diets with those who are eating animal food, the grain- and vegetable-eaters have lower rates of chronic disease.

A fourth principle is to acknowledge and accommodate dietary traditions. In the Bible we read, "give us this day our daily bread." Bread is symbolic of grain itself. Wheat, barley, and other grains were considered the staff of life. In the Far East, rice was considered the staple food, the staff of life. Native Americans respected corn as their staff of life. Wherever you look, no matter what your tradition is, if you go back far enough, you find that your ancestors were eating grains as their principal foods. They used local vegetables and beans as secondary foods. They were eating much less animal food than at present. As people abandoned these traditional eating patterns in favor of the modern diet, their rates of degenerative disease, especially heart disease and cancer, increased dramatically.

Finally, when selecting and preparing daily food, it is important to respect biodiversity, or the tremendous proliferation of life on earth. In nature, biodiversity is the rule, not the exception. To reflect that in our eating, it is important to practice *dietary diversity*. There is a wide proliferation of life on earth, a wide range of species, and to translate that into day-to-day eating, there should be adequate variety in the selection of foods, and also in styles of cooking and food preparation. This principle includes respecting the endless diversity of individual needs. Although all people share certain fundamental things in common, each person is different. Factors such as age, sex, gender, and level of activity, previous diet, cultural background, and others need to be taken into consideration in determining an optimum diet.

LIGHTFOOD GUIDELINES

The guidelines presented below are general suggestions for those living in temperate, or four-season climates. Adjustments are necessary in tropical and semi-tropical, far northern, and Polar climates, as well as for age, gender, activity, and individual needs and preferences.

WHOLE CEREAL GRAINS. At least 50% by weight of every meal is recommended to include cooked, organically grown, whole cereal grains prepared in a variety of ways. Whole cereal grains include brown rice, barley, millet, whole wheat, rye, oats, corn, and buckwheat. A portion of this amount may consist of noodles or pasta, whole grain sourdough breads, and other partially processed whole cereal grains.

SOUPS. Approximately 5-10% of your daily food intake may include soup made with vegetables, sea vegetables (wakame or kombu) grains, or beans. Seasonings are usually miso or shoyu (organic soy sauce) used in moderation.

VEGETABLES. About 25-30% of daily intake may include local and organically grown vegetables. Preferably, the majority is cooked in various styles (e.g., sautéed with a small amount of vegetable oil, steamed, boiled, and sometimes as raw salad or naturally fermented or pickled vegetables. Vegetables for daily use include green cabbage, kale, broccoli, cauliflower, collards, pumpkin, watercress, Chinese cabbage, bok choy, dandelion, mustard greens daikon greens, scallion, onion, daikon, turnip, various fall and summer squashes, burdock, and carrot. Pickled vegetables made without sugar or strong spice, including organic sauerkraut, pickled Chinese cabbage, and others may be eaten on a daily basis.

BEANS AND SEA VEGETABLES. Approximately 5-10% of the daily diet may include cooked beans and sea vegetables. Beans for regular use include azuki, chickpea, lentil, and black soybean, as well as kidney, navy, black bean, white beans, pinto, non-GMO soybean, and others. Bean products such as tofu, tempeh, and natto can also be used.

Sea vegetables such as wakame, nori, kombu, hiziki, arame, dulse, agar, and others may be prepared in a variety of ways. They can be cooked with beans or vegetables, used in soups, or served separately as side dishes or salads, moderately flavored with brown rice vinegar, sea salt, shoyu, ume plum, and other natural seasonings.

OCCASIONAL FOODS. If needed or desired, 1-3 times a week, approximately 10% of the consumption of food can include fresh wild caught flaky white meat fish. Fish and seafood, as well as other forms of animal food, are highly concentrated forms of sunlight. Cold water fishes, for example, contain sunshine synthesized Vitamin D. Animal products were traditionally eaten as a part of an ecological diet as we approach the poles and move away from a strongly sun-energized environment, especially where there is miminum sunlight for many months of the year. Animal foods can be considered optional, transitional, or reserved for occasional use based on need and desire.

Fruit or fruit desserts, including fresh, dried, and cooked fruits, may also be served three or four times per week on average. Local and organically grown fruits are preferred. If you live in a temperate climate, avoid tropical and semi-tropical fruit and eat, instead, temperate climate fruits such as apples, pears, plums, peaches, nectarines, apricots, berries, and melons. Local organic fruit juice may also be consumed.

Lightly roasted nuts and seeds such as pumpkin, sesame, and sunflower may be enjoyed as snacks, together with peanuts, walnuts, almonds, and pecans.

Rice syrup, barley malt, amasake, and mirin may be used as sweeteners, together with occasional maple syrup. Brown rice vinegar, lemon, or umeboshi vinegar may be used for a sour taste.

BEVERAGES. Recommended daily beverages include bancha (kukicha) twig tea, stem tea, roasted brown rice and barley tea, and occasional dandelion and corn silk tea. Any traditional tea that does not have an aromatic fragrance or a stimulating effect can be used. You may also drink a comfortable amount of water (preferably spring or well water of good quality) at room temperature or slightly chilled.

ADDITIONAL SUGGESTIONS. Cooking oil should be vegetable quality only, with natural cold pressed olive and sesame as preferred varieties.

Salt should be naturally processed sea salt. Traditional, non-chemical shoyu or tamari soy sauce and miso may be used as seasonings.

Recommended condiments include:

— Gomashio (sesame salt made from approximately 20 parts roasted sesame seeds to one part sea salt)
— Sea vegetable powder or flakes, including green nori, dulse, kelp, wakame and others, as well as combinations or blends
— Sesame seed wakame powder
— Umeboshi plum
— Tekka
— Roasted seeds such as sunflower or pumpkin

THE CAMBRIDGE DECLARATION ON CONSCIOUSNESS*

On this day of July 7, 2012, a prominent international group of cognitive neuroscientists, neuropharmacologists, neurophysiologists, neuroanatomists and computational neuroscientists gathered at The University of Cambridge to reassess the neurobiological substrates of conscious experience and related behaviors in human and non-human animals. While comparative research on this topic is naturally hampered by the inability of non-human animals, and often humans, to clearly and readily communicate about their internal states, the following observations can be stated unequivocally:

- The field of consciousness research is rapidly evolving. Abundant new techniques and strategies for human and non-human animal research have been developed. Consequently, more data is becoming readily available, and this calls for a periodic reevaluation of previously held preconceptions in this field. Studies of non-human animals have shown that homologous brain circuits correlated with conscious experience and perception can be selectively facilitated and disrupted to assess whether they are in fact necessary for those experiences. Moreover, in humans, new non-invasive techniques are readily available to survey the correlates of consciousness.

- The neural substrates of emotions do not appear to be confined to cortical structures. In fact, subcortical neural networks aroused during affective states in humans are also critically important for generating emotional behaviors in animals. Artificial arousal of the same brain regions generates corresponding behavior and feeling states in both humans and non-human animals. Wherever in the brain one evokes instinctual emotional behaviors in non-human animals, many of the ensuing behaviors are consistent with

179

experienced feeling states, including those internal states that are rewarding and punishing. Deep brain stimulation of these systems in humans can also generate similar affective states. Systems associated with affect are concentrated in subcortical regions where neural homologies abound. Young human and non- human animals without neocortices retain these brain-mind functions. Furthermore, neural circuits supporting behavioral/electrophysiological states of attentiveness, sleep and decision making appear to have arisen in evolution as early as the invertebrate radiation, being evident in insects and cephalopod mollusks (e.g., octopus).

- Birds appear to offer, in their behavior, neurophysiology, and neuroanatomy a striking case of parallel evolution of consciousness. Evidence of near human-like levels of consciousness has been most dramatically observed in African grey parrots. Mammalian and avian emotional networks and cognitive microcircuitries appear to be far more homologous than previously thought. Moreover, certain species of birds have been found to exhibit neural sleep patterns similar to those of mammals, including REM sleep and, as was demonstrated in zebra finches, neurophysiological patterns, previously thought to require a mammalian neocortex. Magpies in particular have been shown to exhibit striking similarities to humans, great apes, dolphins, and elephants in studies of mirror self-recognition.

- In humans, the effect of certain hallucinogens appears to be associated with a disruption in cortical feedforward and feedback processing. Pharmacological interventions in non-human animals with compounds known to affect conscious behavior in humans can lead to similar perturbations in behavior in non-human animals. In humans, there is evidence to suggest that awareness is correlated with cortical activity, which does not exclude possible contributions by subcortical or early cortical processing, as in visual awareness. Evidence that human and non-human animal emotional feelings arise from homologous subcortical brain networks provide compelling evidence for evolutionarily shared primal affective qualia.

We declare the following: "The absence of a neocortex does not appear to preclude an organism from experiencing affective states. Convergent evidence indicates that non-human animals have the neuroanatomical, neurochemical, and neurophysiological substrates of conscious states along with the capacity to exhibit intentional behaviors. Consequently, the weight of evidence indicates that humans are not unique in possessing the neurological substrates that generate consciousness. Non-human animals, including all mammals and birds, and many other creatures, including octopuses, also possess these neurological substrates."

*The Cambridge Declaration on Consciousness was written by Philip Low and edited by Jaak Panksepp, Diana Reiss, David Edelman, Bruno Van Swinderen, Philip Low and Christof Koch. The Declaration was publicly proclaimed in Cambridge, UK, on July 7, 2012, at the Francis Crick Memorial Conference on Consciousness in Human and non-Human Animals, at Churchill College, University of Cambridge, by Low, Edelman and Koch. The Declaration was signed by the conference participants that very evening, in the presence of Stephen Hawking, in the Balfour Room at the Hotel du Vin in Cambridge, UK.

GROWING RICE IN NEW ENGLAND*

Edward Esko
Introduction to the Rice Panel

Before we introduce the members of our panel, I would like to make a few comments about the importance of what they are doing. This is one of the biggest revolutions to occur in America since its founding or even before that. The idea that rice can grow in our robust four-season climate is indeed revolutionary. We have tried over the years to cultivate rice here in the Berkshires, but the seed that we had was from Lundberg Farms in northern California, a mild climate with plenty of sunshine and fresh snowmelt from the Sierra Nevada. So, the rice in the backyard grew, but toward autumn it did not form complete heads. My takeaway from that was that the rice was not hardy enough for our short growing season. But these gentlemen [referring to panelists] have obtained seed from cold climates like Hokkaido in northern Japan and the Ukraine in Europe. That rice is hardy and capable of adapting and growing in this rigorous climate. And this is indeed a revolution. That means that if rice can grow here, it can grow anywhere. That means the entire United States, more or less, maybe exempting the desert and high mountains, is open for rice cultivation.

Now, brown rice is a very special food. I call it the food of our past, and by that I include all cereal grains. By eating brown rice and other whole grains, our ancestors developed unique human characteristics. For example, please notice the delicate hair-like structures that project out from the top of each grain. You can see them on this photo [shows illustration.] This is a photo of Scottish barley, and like rice and other grains, it has these beautiful hair-like structures. These structures are called "awns." What do the awns remind you of? These are actually tiny antennae that point toward the cosmos, toward the universe. As our ancient ancestors started eating these foods, they stood up straight and began to see, visualize, imagine, and commune with the entire universe—the only species on the planet to be able to do that. Of course, later they added fire, cooking, and salt, which made the energy of these foods even more powerful.

Brown rice and other whole grains are also the food of the future because they are conducting and channeling universal cosmic force. During the day, that force is coming primarily from the sun, solar energy, and at night, it is coming from the stars and the universe beyond. By the way, have you seen the research stating that most of the planet, most of North America, is suffering from light pollution? They [referring to scientists] did a map of the world showing the areas that are the most light-polluted and discovered that light pollution is blocking energy from the universe, especially from the Milky Way. How about you [directed to the panelists]? I am sure you are seeing the Milky Way where you live, especially in rural Maine and Vermont. Like the entire planet a century ago, there is little competing artificial light.

Light and energy from the Milky Way plays a direct role in human consciousness and spirituality. In the future that energy will come directly over the North Pole, charging the planet, and that will herald the beginning of a New Age, an Age of Paradise and planetary health and peace. That energy, which grains channel directly through awns, and store deep within the grain like a microchip, that spiritual force is available now to those who base their diet on brown rice and other whole grains. In a sense whole grain eaters are living in the Age of Paradise, similar to the Golden Age of the past. Another Golden Age is coming and those who are fortunate enough to be eating rice and other whole grains, and those who are growing and communing with them, are dealing with, seeing, and experiencing that energy of the future.

The members of today's panel are true pioneers, paving the way toward a sustainable future beginning with the most basic thing, our daily food and growing that most important food, locally, regionally. Our hope is that what they have started here will spread, from the northeastern United States toward the Midwest, Mid-Atlantic, Southern and Plains States, and across the entire United States. Like the Union Pacific railroad, linking East and West, our hope is that the organic rice fields spreading West from New England will link up with those in Lundberg Farms and other growers in California. That will transform the culture, landscape, health, and ecology of the nation and set the stage for a peaceful and sustainable future. I'd like to now introduce our panelists and ask them to share their remarkable stories.

Erik Andrus
Boundbrook Farm

I am honored to be here and to be part of what I think is a fairly important movement. I got into farming in the first place because of my belief in grains and the centrality of grain to sustainable human culture. Originally, I had no idea I was going to end up being a rice farmer. I was mostly inspired by the folklore that went along with wheat and barley. I don't know, I used to be very into folk music and there were a lot of songs about milling wheat and John Barleycorn. I was very into that. I imagined myself as being a farmer who was going to grow grain and process that grain into something that was ready for people to use and that was going to have that whole circle of life fascination with it. When I actually ended up getting a piece of land, I was at that point 34 years old and I looked at this farm which was a piece of Champlain Valley clay farmland, basically pretty flat and open. I decided I was going to do an operation where I was going to crop my own wheat, mill the wheat and bake bread. The land thwarted my vision for it. While perhaps at one time the Champlain Valley grew a lot of wheat, something about the wheat has changed or something about the climate has changed and my crops were often of inferior quality.

I don't want to go too far into it, only I began to be disillusioned with wheat. In 2010, I became familiar with Takeshi Akogi's work. Meanwhile, Christian [referring to Christian Elwell] was growing rice all this time, but I didn't know about him. I knew about Takeshi because he and Linda [his wife] got a SARE [Sustainable Agriculture Research and Education] grant. I attended a workshop about growing rice that Takeshi gave in February 2011. I decided right then that I was going to drop everything I was doing with European cereals and I was going to grow rice.

Sixteen years ago, I lived in Japan for a little over a year. I saw rice growing in Japan and I saw rice being celebrated through the many festivals and the different stages of rice growing. There is a holiday in Japan where everyone gets a long weekend and you are supposed to go and help a rice farmer plant rice. Not everyone does, but that's the reason the holiday exists—to encourage you to go back to your village and help someone plant rice. Anyway, I am not Japanese and I have to say, I wasn't totally in love with whole experience of living in Japan, but part of me was envious that my culture, my people—northeastern United States, New England people, do not have those kinds of touchstones and I feel we need them to survive.

Anyway, I heard about Takeshi's and Linda's work, a light went off and I decided I was going to try to bring about this vision—to bring a whole grain food from start to finish to peoples' tables, but with rice instead of the grains I had thought.

I have been growing rice, this has been our sixth year and we've been ramping up a little bit year-to-year with a few setbacks along the way. There are plenty of things to do wrong as a rice farmer and we have done a lot of them. My goal was and still is to be a "C student" rice farmer by Japanese standards. There are no training wheels; there is no establishment support and if you have a problem with your crop or whatever, then Extension [referring to agricultural extension programs] has no idea how to help, they don't know anything about this. And the other rice growing regions in the United States are so out of scale with what we are doing in the northeast that most of the time the answers they have wouldn't apply anyway—even if they are willing to take the time to talk to us.

California has a non-collaboration policy with non-California growers. If you call most California places, they will practically hang up on you if they find out you are calling from out of state. So we are very much, all three of us here—we are working without a map, very exposed, but I am not discouraged and now after investing all of my money, blood and sweat into this for six years, things are starting to come together. I am hoping for four to six thousand pounds this year, but knock on wood; it's not over until it's over. There are a lot of challenges getting the equipment, the varieties, the soil preparation and to top it all off, we use this method where we manage ducks for weed control—so the ducks swim in amongst the paddies. Weed control emerged as a very serious issue for us, so getting this method right is really important.

Last year, I went back to Japan and met with Takao Furuno who is the leader of the duck-rice movement which is one of the key ecological rice growing movements in Japan and I participated in the 2015 Japanese

Duck-Rice Farming Conference and was very well received there. Farmers there, the ecological small-scale community-minded farmers were delighted to hear about—what the likes of the three of us are doing, amazed and delighted because Japan is very insular and they don't have a lot of ideas about what is happening in ecological rice growing in other countries. So, that was a great experience.

A Japanese rice paddy is really, really shallow, very precisely engineered. So, that's our logo: the diving duck. If you can read Japanese [he reads Japanese characters]: "inside stream rice." So "Boundbrook" [the name of his farm] is like inside stream. That's our mission. "Our mission is to grow staff-of-life foods for ourselves and our neighbors. We are dedicated to a human-scale farming future that works in cooperation with nature." That's our website [referring to www.vermontrice.net] that I just finished working on. I am selling rice from the 2016 harvest through that website now, so that's something I can offer.

If you go to that website, you can buy the rice now. Currently, we are only offering pick up in Ferrisburgh [location of farm in Vermont.] I may be able to arrange some sort of satellite pickup, but what's on the table now is—you have to come to the farm and get it. It would probably be worth the trip because you could see a real full-blown rice farm with paddies and processing equipment and everything.

Edward Esko: Erik can you show us where you are located?
Erik: Sure. [Drawing map of Vermont on board.] Here's Canada up here, New Hampshire, Maine, and Massachusetts, Rhode Island, and New York-achusetts. [Laughter from audience.] Anyway, here's Lake Champlain [pointing to Lake Champlain on map he drew] and I'm right about here [location south of Lake Champlain], so about a 3-hour drive. I'm midway between Burlington and Middlebury. Burlington is here and Middlebury here. We are relatively close to the lake so this is actually one of the warmest spots in the whole state. Once you get down to southern Vermont—for the most part, you are higher altitude so we generally have a warmer growing zone near the lake than folks down further south.

There are so many reasons why I am excited about growing rice. It's really hard to limit it to just a few. Takeshi in his presentation estimated that there were 60,000 acres of marginal poorly drained agricultural land in the Champlain Valley that would be suitable candidates to convert to rice paddies. I don't know how he came up with that figure, but if you just drive down the road, you can see marshy agricultural fields where farmers can barely cut hay in a dry year. Those are the kinds of places where we could be building rice farms of the future. This is what we are all about. Rice paddies do not erode so the classic blight of modern agriculture, that is soil depletion, does not apply to rice paddies. Rice paddies are an artificial wetland and they have the same benefits as natural wetlands including wildlife, flood mitigation.

Ours is a community-oriented model. We want to be there for our neighbors and region first—before profit. We are rebuilding some knowledge and taking what we can from Japanese knowledge and adapting it in our own way. This is not an exact replication of what they do in Japan; it's a repurposing. I did these slides for a Japanese audience, but to compare—rice is grown in California and the Deep South [pointing to a map of the United States.] There is a cluster of long grain rice growing in the Carolinas that has been around since the Colonial times, but those are, for the most part, much larger in scale than what we are doing. This [pointing to map of the northeastern United States] was for the benefit of my Japanese friends to show them where experimental rice farms are located with an arrow for my site. I don't know exactly where Christian's [referring to panelist Christian Elwell] farm is, but I tried to approximate it on the map. You get the idea—that there are people out there trying this. The range at which these things could be done is much, much greater.

There are reasons why we believe in duck and rice farming. It is very efficient; it is stable. The duck in the rice paddy can eliminate both the need for fertilizer and pesticides, herbicides in one stroke and it's beautiful. I don't know how much time I should take up with this, but when I was at the Japanese Duck-Rice Conference, Takao Furuno was asked by someone in the Japanese media: "Why is this kind of farming important? Why should anyone care about it?" If we were at an American farming conference, the answer to that question would have been a tirade about GMOs and Monsanto and the evils of global agriculture and soil depletion and all these things that are very big and abstract.

I've been to a lot of these conferences and they get very political. So, I was kind of expecting Takao Furuno to say something about that—it's your life's work, why does it matter. Instead, his answer was this: "When I was a kid, my dad farmed rice in the usual way. He wasn't organic, but chemicals weren't around in those days. He would take me out to the fields to help him plant rice or whatever he was doing and I was just a little kid and not very much help. I would get bored or tired and I would help sometimes, as long as I could, but when I would stop being useful, my dad would say 'Go play.' And I would go and play in the irrigation ditches beside the rice paddy and I would find all kinds of salamanders, frogs, and sometimes a turtle or a snake. I learned all the little places where these creatures would live."

"That is how I passed my hours. I wasn't really with my dad, but he was in the field right there so I felt close to him and I spent all these hours looking for these little animals. When I grew up, I went to college and got a job working in an office, but I didn't like doing that. I kept thinking about these happy memories I had as a kid, looking for all these creatures. When my dad died and I inherited the rice farm, that was one of the things that bonded me to the place, made me want to come back and begin farming rice."

"When I started farming rice, I did it the way everyone told me to do and that involved using chemicals. When I looked for these creatures in the ditches, they were not there. They weren't in my field and they weren't in my neighbors' fields either. Then, I started to experiment, little by little, with duck-rice farming. As I stopped using chemicals, little by little the animals came back. When I had children, without being told 'Go look for animals in the irrigation ditches,' they found them the same way I did when I was a kid. Now, my grandkids, too, they love to play in the water and look for animals. So, it seems to me, if there was more duck-rice farming in the world, then maybe kids would want to be rice farmers. They would come back to the village where they were born and they would want to farm rice."

All of this is such an emotional argument. A lot of the village people were practically weeping by the end of it, without once mentioning global agriculture—like why industrial agriculture is bad and why this is good. Anyway, that's Takao Furuno, a very interesting guy. It was a real honor to meet him. Anyway, I have a bunch more stuff. This is sort of the remnant of a technical presentation of how to create rice projects which is one of the things I am starting to get into now. I was actually involved in helping create Ben Rooney's [Ben is one of the panelists] project in Maine, so some of the sucker punches that we took along the way creating rice farming systems have been informative enough that I can sometimes spare other people those same sucker punches. That seems to be service worth rendering. Anyway, if you are curious about how a paddy system works [referring to diagram on next page] and how it differs from a natural landform, here's a little diagram about how you would go about creating a paddy system on a typical piece of land.

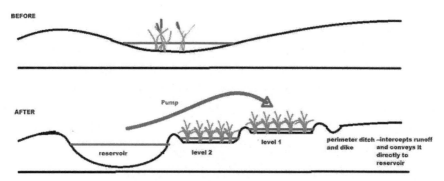

Paddy System. A perimeter ditch redirects water around your project area and fills the reservoir when it rains. The paddiy should gravity drain easily from highest to lowest to the reservoir. It's important to be able to raise or lower water levels at will

You start with something that has a flowing gradient to it and pick levels. Each paddy is like a baking sheet—it's flat in the middle and has a lip around it. You have to have some means of controlling water. It's one of the main jobs of a rice farmer—regulating water levels according to the needs of the crop. This is the system. These [referring to photo] are rice ducks and they spend 24/7 in the rice paddies and they maneuver around; they are small enough to get in between the plants.

Question from audience: What do they eat?
Erik: Actually, these are crossbreed ducks. They swim through the paddy and they eat snails and weeds and bugs and all kinds of things. In the process, a handful of rice plants get knocked over, but that is more than outweighed by the benefits—that's more than balanced by the stabilization—by muddying the water, they help the rice plants pick up nutrients to a much greater degree, making the system very productive. So, the water is always muddy.

Question from audience: Do you feed them at all?
Erik: I feed them a little bit just to maintain control over them. They always come when I call. Anyway, this [referring to a slide], this is my own farm here. This is in Ferrisburgh, Vermont. This is from last year. I'm releasing the ducks from this duck transporter that we built and there they all go.

Question from audience: How many ducks do you have?
Erik: It's about a hundred [referring to the quantity of ducks] per acre. This year, we started with four hundred and some are always lost to predators. This is also in Japan [referring to slide.] These ducks are crossbreeds. They have a mallard parent and a Khaki Campbell parent as well. Eventually, I would like to get to where I am breeding my own ducks, but currently I am just buying purebred Khaki Campbells. They are as happy as can be.

Question from audience: How much time do they spend in the rice paddy?
Erik: Their time in the rice paddy is relatively short. They are in the rice paddy for six weeks or so. That's the period between when the rice is transplanted and when it is beginning to go to seed. The magic of duck and rice farming is that ducks don't eat rice leaves because rice leaves contain silica, but they will eat rice grain—so you have to remove the ducks from the field before the rice grain matures. So that gives you a window of about six weeks when the ducks are very useful. In our case, we introduce the ducks to the field on about June 20th and they came out on August 8th.

Question from audience: How do you get them out?
Erik: I say "Duck, duck, duck" and they all come out.

Question from audience: Where are they going?
Erik: Actually, this year's ducks—of all things, a vegan perma-culturist lady bought the ducks from me to help clean up her orchards. Now she is a vegan perma-culturist animal farmer. Anyway, she intends to let the ducks live out the natural course of their lives on her estate. It was a good deal. I was able to sell the ducklings for something and she gets ducklings to help with her orchards.

Illustrations by: Boundbrook Farm

Christian Elwell
South River Farm

We moved to Conway, Massachusetts in 1979—to South River Farm. The South River runs through our property; that's how it's named. Back in the 1970s, I first had the impulse to want to grow rice—it came out of Michio Kushi's International Macrobiotic Congress held in Brookline, Massachusetts. The Congress was actually a group of friends getting together and discussing what we were doing and what we might want to do—looking at a future way of life, wherever we were living.

I was on the Agricultural Committee and back in those days—it may seem commonplace now—we started talking about what it would be like if we had local sources for our food. Many macrobiotic friends were eating seaweed and umeboshi plums from Japan and rice from California. So, what if we could grow rice in New England? When we purchased our farm in Conway, one of the first things I did, even before starting the miso company—was to grow the different grains: barley, oats, rye, wheat, corn, and millet in small plots—because I wanted to see them grow. I wanted to experience them as plants. When I grew up my father had a vegetable farm, and I also worked on a dairy farm as a kid. I had a lifelong connection with plants, but I didn't have any connection with the cereal grains. I wanted to experience them as living plants.

I didn't grow rice at first because I thought, "Oh, you can't grow rice in New England." That was the common mindset. Then in the early 1980s, I heard that there was an agronomist at Cornell University where I had gone to school who had been growing rice, John Peverly. I wrote to him and asked for some seed that I might be able to try it out. He sent a small amount of seed, two varieties: one was medium-grain rice from Italy, and the other was a short grain variety from the Ukraine. I planted out these seeds, maybe fifty or so seeds at most, of each variety, and immediately, after they came into flower, I was attracted to the rice from the Ukraine, because it had these wonderful, amazing awns, whereas the Italian rice did not have awns.

It was obvious to me that these awns are like antennae; they are actually receptors, organs for receiving cosmic influence, for receiving the 'divine

194

plan,' so to speak, radiating from the stars. You watch the plant as it grows upward and these receptors, these awns, go reaching up and out toward the cosmos, towards the formative light forces of sun, moon, and stars.

Transplanting rice in the paddy

You can observe in the morning and evening as drops of dew congeal out of the surrounding star-lit atmosphere and form droplets of water on the awns as well as on the leaves and other parts of the plant. In my imagination, I felt that the rice, going through all these life stages of growth and reaching out with these delicate receptors, these awns, to the heavens—and the dew congealing out of the atmosphere on the delicate hairs of these awns— in my imagination it was clear that each single grain of rice is born out of the Cosmos, as a child of the Cosmic Whole.

The grain, at first an empty flower, fills up with milk-like *manna* from the starry heavens, which then ripens and hardens under the September sun and eventually forms what we know and eat (!) as the grain of rice. In the beginning it is liquid milk—called milk because it is a white liquid. In my imagination, this white liquid is formed and informed out of the dew that collects on the awns that are in touch with the etheric atmosphere of the environment permeated, as it is, with cosmic influences.

Later, when I talked with a rice breeder from Cornell about this, I asked her what role the awns play in the development of a grain of rice. She said the awns don't have anything to do with it, because when the plant breeders snip off the awns—which they do when they are hybridizing the rice—the grain still develops. "So the awns must not really be necessary," so she thought. I said, in effect, "I wish you would research this more thoroughly; check it out. Because it seems to me that the formative forces creating and informing the grain milk come down through the receptor-awns to the base of the flower, where the ovary is located.

The ovary fills with grain milk, eventually forming the seed, this single, unique grain of rice." She said she would like to research this, but I don't think the powers that be would fund such research.

It challenges the whole idea of modern plant breeding, of seed manipulation at the core of agribusiness, which actually separates the plant from its cosmic origins *and,* consequently, separates us from our cosmic nutrition.

I was able to find some research done on the awns in wheat where they have shown that the awns actually photosynthesize light and that they do play a role in the formation of the grain, in this case, of wheat.

One does not need to be a scientist to carefully notice and observe these things. In fact, it may be the innocent eyes of a child that can more easily see what the awns signify. They are not irrelevant appendages. Some say the awns exist to protect the grain from hungry, attacking birds. But in my experience the awns do not bother the birds at all. The birds come and are very happy to eat the rice with or without awns; the awns do not deter them.

My interest in growing rice has been more of a poetic, scientific interest—I would say a spiritual scientific interest—rather than a commercial scientific interest.

I have had the good fortune of a livelihood from the miso company [referring to his company, South River Miso] and growing rice has never been a commercial interest for me. I wanted to find out first, could rice be grown in New England and the northeast? Secondly, I wanted to get to know the nature of the rice plant in its native, heirloom quality and to develop a pure relationship with it free of commercial interest.

Erik [referring to Erik Andrus] was mentioning that there is not a lot of support for growing rice in New England. I can testify to that as well. In the 1980s, growing little plots of rice, it was an extremely difficult undertaking, and especially to overcome the thought forms then prevailing. The preconception that you cannot grow rice in New England was not easy to overcome. But this preconception is now a proven misconception and is mostly to do with commercial concerns, whether it is commercially feasible. It does not have to do with horticultural or biological limitations. Rice itself as a plant, will grow in New England, as I have now proven in Conway for over 30 years, for over 30 generations of rice, carrying the seed from each generation to the next.

There were a couple of years when I planted only ten grains and had only ten plants to take care of. I had a family and business to take care of, too, so I needed to keep the rice project in bounds. There was a long period of time, when it was a great effort to plant a few seeds, period. I only sensed in my heart that the rice wanted to grow here, and I wanted to watch it grow and become familiar with it as a plant. And year-by-year it acclimated to the environment.

For many years I grew the rice by the dry land method, until I saw Takeshi Akaogi's rice paddy in Putney, Vermont. Takeshi had been visiting our place over the years, giving me tips about growing rice. He had grown rice in Japan and had lived and worked with Masanobu Fukuoka. Finally, after his children were grown, Takeshi planted his own rice paddy in Putney.

When I visited there, I realized immediately that the rice paddy is more than about growing rice. It is a whole ecosystem of living organisms *and* plants growing together. Frogs, salamanders, newts, pollywogs, and dragonflies, even turtles… they and many other creatures all live there! In my own youth, I lived near swamps and fields, streams and ponds. I used to catch pollywogs and watch them become frogs. So, to see the frogs and salamanders and dragonflies and all of these things, living in and attracted to Takeshi's rice paddy, was a very exciting experience for me.

The very next year I created our own rice paddy right in front of our home in Conway. And that very first year, I heard a sound at night that I had never heard before, after 30 years of living there. [Christian makes a whirling sound.] That's a bad imitation! When I first heard it, it sounded to me like a tropical bird.

Close up of rice grains with awns

I thought a tropical bird must have escaped from someone's home. I tracked it down at night with a flashlight and thanks to an audio clip online; I discovered it was the gray tree frog, an astonishing creature.[1] This is not the spring peeper; it's a different frog. The adult is about this size [shows size by making a circle with his thumb and 2nd finger]; the adult has chameleon-like properties and can change its color according to the background. It is very attracted to shallow vernal pools, like the rice paddy, to lay its

---

1 Google 'gray tree frog', or see the video https://www.youtube.com/watch?v=9bzotS1ow0Q

eggs—so some of these gray tree frogs came to the rice paddy and laid their eggs that very first year. Now their progeny come in droves every year to fill our neighborhood with their festive song.

One of the most wonderful experiences—and I shared this last Monday night at my presentation [referring to his Summer Conference lecture the Monday evening prior], was coming out one morning just as the rice was coming into flower, which I knew was a very special time in the life of the rice plant, and I wanted to be there for it. I saw some of the flowers emerging from the stalk [moves to the rice plant displayed in the front of the room and touches the plant.] Each one of these stalks is called a tiller and when the flower head first emerges, it is as if it peers up out of the stalk and then emerges like a baby from the womb. It then elongates and extends and becomes the flowering head—in botanical terms, the panicle. When it first emerges, it's kind of bundled up, womb-like, and it slowly emerges out of the stalk.

When I saw these first flowering panicles emerging, I ran back into the house to get a camera to photograph this. And as I went around the paddy looking for all the emerging panicles, I was astonished by what I saw next. On one rice plant I saw a dragonfly nymph that had climbed up out of the rice paddy waters during the night. And out of this nymph, it's shell, was now emerging a beautiful dragonfly, which then rested on top of the discarded shell, expanding and drying its wings, preparing for takeoff as a totally new phenomenon, a creature of air. I said to myself, "Wow, that's amazing. This is happening at the same time the rice is coming into flower!"

Then I looked around some more and noticed tiny green, baby tree frogs that had also climbed up out of the paddy onto the rice leaves during the night, emerging out of their pollywog existence in the water. They were perched on the rice leaves, acclimating to their new environment of the air, and their new life as terrestrial creatures. They would remain there, perched on the rice leaves for two or three days and then venture off into the wild world around them—leaving behind their water-life as pollywogs.

This was such a powerful experience for me in my relationship with the rice. In that single morning everything conspired in a brilliant way to show me—which I now share with you—what the rice coming into flower—it's true of any plant coming into flower—just what the flowering stage represents in the life of the plant. When a plant comes into flower, it is equivalent to the nymph changing into the dragonfly, or the pollywog changing into the frog, or the caterpillar changing into the butterfly. It awakened me to the enormity in the plant's life of what it means to come into flower. And it awakened me more deeply into our own story as human beings. For we too are creatures of change and self-transformation. Amazing things can happen when we as human beings participate in, and bear witness to the life of the plants that, in turn, nourish us.

Erik was talking about his experience in Japan—where in the traditional culture there, the plant and the life stages of the rice are as much a part of the cultural life experience of the people, especially in traditional cultures. The food and medicinal plants are recognized and treated with reverence and gratitude through ritual and ceremony, just as the different stages of human life—for instance—Bar Mitzvah or birthdays or special rites of passage are recognized in the community. The traditional spiritual and cultural life of the human community includes the food and medicinal plants and the different phases that the plants go through. You find this with Native Americans with the corn, the celebrations and rituals around the different stages in the life of the corn plant. We cannot overestimate what this means in the life and co-evolution of a people with their sources of food and medicine. Wherever the plants are honored and held within the minds and hearts of the people, this makes a huge difference in what the plants are able to bring forth in return.

One day, several years ago, I was planting the rice seed. When I first plant the rice, I plant it in seed flats after soaking the seeds and starting the seedlings in a greenhouse. Then I plant the rice to its permanent location outdoors toward the middle or end of May. Rice is not frost hardy, so you have to plant the rice after all danger of frost has passed. So, I was in the process of putting the soaked seed into the seed flats when, out of the blue, without any warning, a fellow named Bob Carr, an old macrobiotic friend and teacher from Ohio—stopped by to say hello. I hadn't seen him for twenty-five years.

I said "Wow, Bob, this is an amazing synchronicity, that you have come at this particular moment. We can plant the rice seeds together." And he said, "Have you read *Anastasia*?" I said, "Who is Anastasia?" "You have to read her book before you can plant the rice," he said. "But Bob, I have only this time to plant the rice," I said. "I've got to do it today. Can you give me a few highlights; sum it up for me?" And, so, he did.

Anastasia is a legendary healer who lives in Siberia; there are some books written about her and her teachings. She gives a profound picture of our food plants and how we have lost connection to them. She also gives some suggestions for what we can do to start to remedy this. Bob shared all of this with me, namely, that the plants no longer know what we as human beings need for our evolution and our healing, because we are no longer in touch with them. We no longer know who they are and who we are in relation to them. They no longer know who we are and what we need.

In terms of the ways we think about plants, we usually think of them as "things" or commodities, but they are not "things" at all. They are not commodities any more than people are commodities, at which point they are called slaves.

As soon as we call something like a plant a commodity, we take it out of its living context; we deaden the world and dehumanize ourselves. We then feel free to manipulate the plant, for example, according to our need or greed, because it is only a "thing."

It's radical and amazing to start holding plants as companions, as honored friends, as fellow travelers, even as elders who have a rightful place alongside us in this world, indeed, as elders who have something to offer us for the journey we are making together, for our mutual healing and well-being. Plants can nourish us with the cosmic forces of nutrition we need for our evolution only if they know who we are and what we need, and only if we regard them in a similar way, and bring ourselves into an ongoing living and loving connection with them.

Anastasia says that the modern plants have lost touch with us—they have been outwardly manipulated, bred, or modified according to materialistic thought forms of a civilization that has forgotten the sacred and lost its way. Plants are bred for quantity yields, for economic and commercial efficiencies. But the plants themselves *as beings* are not seen. Thus abused, they are less present and can no longer know or serve who we are. We need to honor ourselves and honor them. We need to make them part of new ceremonies and rituals, to carry them in our hearts again.

So, Anastasia makes this simple yet profound recommendation to address the question: what can we do to bring ourselves back into relationship with our food bearing and medicinal plants? And this is the practice she recommends, in short: take the seeds and put them in your mouth for nine minutes and during that time, the being of the plant registers your being, takes in "information" from you as a human being in the silent *interbeingness* between you and the plant.

Then, breathe on the seeds, and hold the seeds between your palms before your heart and, before planting them, hold them in your hands beneath the whole cosmos, and then, finally, you plant them in the soil.

This way, through this simple ritual, you bring yourself into a profound relationship with the plant.[2] When Bob described this to me, I thought, "What a beautiful practice! Let's do it!" And I asked him, "How am I going to put three thousand seeds in my mouth?" He said, "You don't have to place every seed in your mouth. Just take a few and they will communicate with the others what they know of you." So that is what we did, and I have been practicing this little ritual every year since.

What I noticed in that first year, which astounded me really—and I can't say how it has affected the rice—all I can say is how it has affected me. It changed my sensitivity to the plant. I began to have a relationship with the rice in the same way you might begin to develop a relationship with a human friend—when you first make a connection—you start to exchange stories, start to meet and get to know each other. This little ceremony brought me into a relationship with the rice that was previously hidden or unconscious. The ritual made it conscious, and a world of relationship opened up that continues to inform me and nourish me in ways that I could not have imagined before. Plants nourish us in so many ways

---

2 For complete details of this practice please refer to *Anastasia,* by Vladimir Megré, Ringing Cedars Press, Kahului, Hawaii: 2008, Chapter 11, pages 77-80.

besides eating their material substance. They also nourish us through the exchange that takes place in our thoughts and feelings, our soul and spiritual connection with life.

Of course, there are many ways and practices that can bring us back to our senses, bring us back to reality, to our connection with Life. When we prepare our meals with knowledge and love, when we eat our meals with gratitude and thanksgiving, we are also bringing ourselves back into relationship with the plants and with the cosmos that has brought us into manifestation.

But we cannot leave the plants themselves outside the circle of our awareness. Anastasia urges us on, and points out another step as we seek wholeness, as we seek connection with the plants themselves as the source of our food and medicine. This is what I wanted to share with you.

Photos: South River Miso Co.

Christian Elwell is the founder/owner of South River Miso Company in Conway, Massachusetts.

Edward Esko

Wild Folk Farm
Ben Rooney

There's a lot of overlap with what these two fellows just said. Yeah, I got into it—I guess I will start with the touch idea—I feel like I and other people were really out of touch with growing grain. I was interested in the type of farming that was human-powered, being on the soil, on the land—interacting in different ways, whether it was with the crops or anything around. I was working on a farm and tried to grow some wheat. I was using a scythe, the typical grim reaper tool that some people use or used to use—less frequently now to cut hay, to cut grains, and they used to do it in parties or in groups in the common areas. That image, seeing it in a book resonated with me and I guess it talked to me in some spiritual sense. I don't remember a lot of dreams, but I had agreed to be involved with something, there were a lot of scythes being used, an image of a lot of people cutting down grain and there were tools that forced you to do a good job. If you are rushed, if you are not present with what you are doing, it will manifest in what you are doing.

So, I came to this new piece of land and I wanted to grow grains really badly. I wanted it to be all over the state of Maine and I wanted other people to experience growing grain. I really felt there were these myths that grains needed to grow in huge monocultures with big machines. I felt these were disempowering myths and so we started growing some.

We soon learned that the farm was not great for growing most of them [referring to various grains.] There was a reason why the biggest dairies in the state that surrounded our farm didn't buy the land and the reason why my friend bought it was because he was able to get it for a certain price [meaning he negotiated a good deal on the purchase.] It was marginal farming soil, much as Erik was talking about. When we think about growing rice in the future in this area, there are pieces of land like ours that are very wet, that are very high in clay. It's tough to grow a lot of things that we grow, whether it is beets or carrots or tomatoes or wheat or oats—those were some of the grains that I was trying.

204

Seedlings in early May

I was similarly inspired by some of the stuff in Japan, like these two guys [referring to Erik Andrus and Christian Elwell]—so we gave it a try. It felt good on many levels. It felt good on our ten by ten plot—just to see how they would do.

Many of the other crops on the farm required more space, but the rice did pretty well. Being able to walk in a small paddy—when we added water—to see the frogs and tadpoles coming in—we immediately connected that to our land. There were frogs and tadpoles everywhere. Anywhere you dug a hole in the clay, it filled up with water; so, it really turned into some permaculture principles, which are about listening to your land.

We had this small paddy, I saw the rice doing well, and I saw other things flourish in it—so it seemed to make sense to expand. We did some. We followed similar practices; we have ducks in the paddy as well. We tried to get a good amount of water in the paddy; we used certain aquatic plants in the paddy that fix nitrogen, similar to duck weed, except that these plants multiply a lot faster and die at frost.

Reading about this in *The Power of the Duck* book [referring to *The Power of the Duck: Integrated Rice and Duck Farming* by Takao Furuno]—this was before we were growing the rice that I read this book—and I really wanted to give it a try. I was thinking that this is a grain we can grow, this is a grain we can grow on human power because of the water management—it really helps with weeds, because of the ducks, the fertility, and the aquatic plants. It seemed to me that this is a system, maybe it's not a closed loop fully, but more closed than other agricultural systems we have. As Erik's bullet points mentioned [referring to Erik's PowerPoint presentation], it is the most stable and efficient crop system on the planet—reading about that and thinking about that—I was more or less sold to be able to experience it.

It made sense to have this polyculture and to expand into a bigger paddy, to get some ducks. It was the most beautiful thing I have seen in agriculture, seeing those three things and seeing this beauty—you are in there and everything feels serene and you feel as though you have helped create and manifest this ecosystem with wild polyculture and domestic. Yeah, just seeing the water in there and having that stillness, to have the rice grow and to have all the different dragonflies come up—there is something really powerful in that. That, combined with the yields we were getting, inspired us to continue and to grow.

Ducks in the rice paddy

I became really inspired to try lots of different seeds; last year we grew thirty different types of rice. I got a lot of them from the USDA, from all over the world. There is some red rice in there, some long grain; there's some sticky rice, some short grain and they all taste good. The risotto rice we are growing now is doing really well; we grow short grain as well and we are really trying to hone in on how to grow a rice economy in this area [referring to Maine.] We need to think about how to grow it in different places and we need to diversify the different types of rice we are growing. That was definitely something we were doing. Now, we have nine different varieties; we have an acre of rice paddies. They are each an eighth (1/8) of an acre—eight paddies.

Yeah, that's my answer to the question of how we got into it and where we are now. I'm greatly inspired by the human-power aspect of it. We had our first big work party this spring; we had about fifty people come out for transplanting. It's really fun transplanting the rice with three or four people—don't get me wrong—but when you get the paddies at the right muddy consistency, you can transplant them very fast—even just with human power, much faster than other crops. I'll say the same thing about it—if the water levels can be managed without weeds or if the ducks are in there, the weeds come out much faster—so seeing these things happen got me thinking that this was a grain that could do really well in this area. We looked at the State of Maine and found there were two hundred thousand acres where we could grow rice in cleared areas. Getting back to this work party, we had fifty people come out to help transplant rice and it was a really beautiful thing.

As I think about the future, where we are going to have more people involved in growing food as there is less use of machinery, I'm thinking about ways to do that where it is fun, where it's building community, where it feels good, where there are all these different people touching and interacting with this food that they will soon eat. This is really powerful. I remember seeing at one point, forty or fifty people in paddies and they looked so small. Everyone was having such a really good time, just planting the rice and it was so powerful to think about that. It's a great way to get people out looking at wildlife while being in the open air. How can we spread this to other areas? And grains are really great—because there is this huge burst of planting in the spring and in the fall. If you are growing rice paddies, it can really compliment your farm because you can let the water and ducks do their work during the season. That, in itself makes it really conducive to these communal activities.

Photos: Wild Folk Farm

*From the Panel Discussion at the Macrobiotic Summer Conference, August 2016.

AWNED WAVES OF GRAIN
By Alex Jack
President, Planetary Health, Inc.

Awned is the new organic. Awns are the long, thin antennae-like bristles that protrude from the heads of grain growing in the field. The modern diet and health revolution began with macrobiotics a half century ago. First, brown rice was introduced as a healthier alternative to white rice and served as the iconic food of the natural foods movement. Second, organic replaced chemically grown whole grains and other plant-quality foods.

Third, awned rice is on the verge of entering the food supply as the next wave in raising human awareness and creating a sustainable planet. At the Macrobiotic Summer Conference in August, a small amount of awned rice donated by South River Farm was featured at the closing Gala. Then at the Thanksgiving celebration at Eastover, awned brown rice was served in the main grain dish (mixed with sweet rice and wild rice). Early this winter, the Amber Waves Network (AWN), a division of the nonprofit Planetary Health, Inc., began distributing a small volume of awned rice from Wild Folk Farm in Maine to donors for ceremonial use.

As part of the new rice revolution, organic brown rice is now grown commercially for the first time in Maine, Vermont, Massachusetts, New York, New Jersey, and other Eastern states. We plan to encourage other farmers to grow awned rice and add it to our new label Lima Rice, named after macrobiotic pioneer Lima Ohsawa, who lived to be 102.

The Legacy of Awned Grain
The colloquial, non-scientific name for awned is "bearded." In the classic description of the Golden Age, the legendary era of universal peace and plenty, the Roman poet Ovid observed: "The spring was everlasting, and gentle zephrs with warm breath played with the flowers that sprang

unplanted. Anon the earth, untilled, brought forth her stores of grain, and the fields, though unfallowed, grew white with the heavy, bearded wheat."

Close up, awns look like facial hair on the growing heads or kernels of grain; hence the name "bearded." They may be short or long, single or multiple, curved or straight. Some grains have long beards, between 4-7 inches. Others are only ½- to 1-inch, virtually stubble. Awnless grains were traditionally known as "beardless" or "bald.

Like antennae, awns gather and absorb the waves and vibrations of the cosmos, including the sun, moon, stars, and distant galaxies. Although the beards are removed—or we might say shaved—during harvest and before eating, the cosmic energy goes into the kernels. When ingested as a whole grain, porridge, bread, or other grain product, that quanta of stored energy shapes and influences our body, mind, and spirit. At night, awns rotate and point downward, also gathering the deep energy of the earth.

Awns also serve a practical function. Their tiny barbs hinder mammals from nibbling, as well as adhere to their fur for propagating. As the grain ripens and naturally falls to earth, the awns serve as rotating blades to drive the seeds deeper into the soil than if they fell flat on the ground. Similarly, during increased humidity at nights, the bristles straighten vertically, twine together, and further push the seed into the soil. During the day, when the humidity drops, the awns open again, and fine silica hairs on the bristles prevent the seeds from reversing direction. In this way, the awns can propel the seed into the earth up to an inch, ensuring that more will germinate.

For most of human existence, our forebears consumed strong, wild awned grains. During periods of high natural electromagnetic radiation, when the Milky Way galaxy was directly overhead (e.g., about 15,000-20,000 years ago), the enhanced energy created an era of abundance and tranquility that was remembered as the time of Paradise. Awned rice, wheat, barley, and other grains were the key to channeling this powerful energy. Meanwhile, as the constellations precessed, the Milky Way dipped lower down in the sky and its energy diminished. Wild grains and other food became scarce, and cultivation began. The significance of awned grains was gradually lost.

With the spread of farming about 10,000 years ago, awnless varieties of grains were selected by early cultivators. These new domesticated awnless strains gave higher yields, required less labor to process, and resulted in a smoother, more uniform product with less spikes, straw, and other residue. Awnless rice was favored in Asia and Africa, and since ancient times Chinese, Indian, and Africa rice (Japonica, Indica, and Glaberrima) were primarily grown without awns.

A small number of awned rice varieties survived, particularly in remote and isolated regions. The type grown by South River and Wild Folk farms is called Duborskian, and comes from Ukraine and Russia. It is a dry land variety, yields beautiful tall plants and long awns, and readily acclimates to temperate climates in North America. "The awns serve like antennae," explains Ben Rooney of Wild Folk. "Watch your harvested drying kernels shoot up towards the sky and rotate, as they are drying or being stored."

Unlike cultivated rice, the long, beautiful yin awns of domesticated barley, wheat, and rye contribute to photosynthesis, produce larger heads, and give higher yields. As a result, awned varieties were favored in the Middle East and Europe and continue to be grown today. The Bible often mentions fresh heads of grain, including "hairy barley" (seorim in Hebrew). Awnless barley is used for making hay. Hard winter wheat, which is used for bread and baked goods and contains the highest amount of protein, is awned and accounts for more than 40% of the U.S. wheat crop. Durum wheat, used for making pasta and noodles, is also awned.

Oats and common yellow millet, known as foxtail millet, have small, yang awns. The name "foxtail" refers to the plant's awns or foxlike brushes. Glutinous millet (broomcorn) tends to have slightly fuller awns as its name suggests. Sorghum comes in both awned and awnless varieties. Maize has soft corn silk, rather than awns, that aid in pollination and will naturally detach when fertilized. Data on awns is not easy to come by, so it's hard to estimate the extent to which any single grain, or the world's grain supply as a whole, is awned.

In some places, awns are actually used in cooking or baking. In Crete, awns are traditionally ground and added to hulled barley to make whole grain bread. The special bread is held to contribute to the country's low cancer rate.

In effect, awned grains are small natural batteries that gather, collect, and charge us with the spiraling energy of heaven and earth. Awnless grains, especially those that are grown organically, still contribute to daily health and well-being. But the strong extra quanta of Ki, or life energy, in awned grains attune us to the higher, deeper frequencies of the cosmos, including universal images of peace, love, beauty, and truth. The incoming energy also helps us to align with larger astronomical cycles of change such as the precession of the equinoxes.

The Centrality of Rice
Cooked grains as a whole shaped and influenced our unique human form and structure, differentiating us from earlier primates who ate primarily raw fruit, seeds, and nuts. Eating wild grasses as main food gave our ancestors flexibility, adaptability, higher consciousness, and the ability to visualize and realize their dreams.

Each type of grain further gives slightly different qualities. Wheat, barley, oats, and rye contribute to creativity, artistry, and adventure. Maize and quinoa lend warmth, passion, and radiance. Millet creates a resourceful, practical mind, as well as sympathy and understanding. Buckwheat gives confidence and will power. Rice develops synthesis, unity, and oneness. In a world divided by competing goals, allegiances, and identities, these unifying qualities are needed more than ever. Compared to other grains, rice lacks a seam in the middle and is the most biologically advanced of all cereal plants.

Eating a balanced plant-based diet, including whole grain rice, is the foundation for planetary health and peace. For half the world, rice is the main staple. It is vital that whole, organic, and awned rice and other grains be consumed as humanity addresses age-old problems related to disease, injustice, and war and constructs a new golden age.

Practical Steps
To optimize your health and consciousness, the following guidelines may be observed:

1. Make whole grains the foundation of your diet.
2. Eat whole grain rice (brown rice) at least once a day. Awnless (short-awned) is fine for daily health and well-being.

3. Obtain a small amount of awned brown rice for ceremonial or meditative purposes until it becomes more widely available for regular use.

4. Eat other awned grains and grain products regularly, especially barley, whole wheat, rye, and spelt that are generally awned. Millet, sorghum, and quinoa are excellent for general health and vitality and may or may not have awns.

5. Keep a food journal and jot down the effects of awned vs. awnless, e.g., how you feel physically, mentally or emotionally, as well as dreams, visions, etc. Several friends who obtained packages of Lima Rice at Planetary Health's Thanksgiving celebration contacted us afterward and said the awned rice was the best they ever ate and enhanced their well-being at many levels.

6. Grow awned rice in your garden or in a bucket on your windowsill or patio. Instructions on how to grow your own rice are available on our website: www.amberwaves.org. Duborskian seeds are available very affordably from Wild Folk Farm www.wildfolkfarm. com/farmstore/riceseed. Google "Duborskian rice" for a complete list of seed suppliers.

7. Educate others about awned grains, distribute copies of *The Rice Revolution* (Amberwaves Press, 2017), and support the Amber Waves Network (AWN).

Source: Amberwaves Newsletter, Winter 2017.

RESOURCES

Macrobiotic Online Course
In this first of its kind course combining video, audio, print and live interaction, students have the opportunity to study all facets of macrobiotics with Edward Esko, Founder of the International Macrobiotic Institute (IMI.) The IMI Online Certificate Course is designed to enable students to gain the full benefit from their daily practice of macrobiotics, while developing the knowledge and skill to guide and counsel others. The IMI also sponsors IMI Press, a publisher of books by Michio Kushi, Edward Esko, Naomi Ichikawa Esko, and other macrobiotic authors. Contact: InternationalMacrobioticInstitute.com.

Planetary Health, Inc.
PHI is the sponsor of the Amber Waves Network (AWN) that led the effort to prevent the introduction of GM rice and wheat in the Unites States. Publisher of the quarterly Amberwaves newsletter and, through Amberwaves Press, books by Edward Esko, Alex Jack, Bettina Zumdick, and others on holistic health, diet, philosophy, and medicine. Current projects include a plant-based diet intervention study for type 2 diabetes, in association with Berkshire Health Systems, and *The Spirit of Rice* Film Documentary. Contact: PlanetaryHealth.com.

Macrobiotic Summer Conference
The annual gathering held in Massachusetts and online that brings together leading teachers, instructors, and guides from around the world for a residential program in the beautiful Berkshire Mountains of Massachusetts or an online event. Sponsored by Planetary Health, Inc. Info at: MacrobioticSummerConference.com.

***Macrobiotics Today*/George Ohsawa Macrobiotic Foundation (GOMF)**
GOMF is a macrobiotic publisher and educational center in Chico, California. *Macrobiotics Today* quarterly features articles by Edward Esko and other macrobiotic authors. Contact: OhsawaMacrobiotics.com.

Audiobooks on Audible
Audible.com has a growing catalogue of Edward Esko books available for download as professionally produced audio files. Visit the Audible website for the list of titles and ordering information. Contact: Audible.com/ Edward Esko.

ABOUT THE AUTHOR

Edward Esko in Dubai

Edward Esko, born in Philadelphia on October 16, 1950, is one of the world's most active contemporary macrobiotic teachers. Over the past four decades, he has lectured and counseled in Europe, Asia, Latin America, the Middle East, and throughout North America, including at the United Nations, and has written and edited numerous books and articles. Building on the teachings of George Ohsawa, Michio Kushi, and other macrobiotic pioneers, he has applied yin and yang—the universal principles of change and harmony—to helping solve issues of personal and planetary health. He has served as Executive Director of the East West Foundation and Director of Education at the Kushi Institute. He is the founder of the International Macrobiotic Institute (IMI) in Massachusetts, and serves on the Board of Planetary Health, Inc., which is the non-profit sponsor of the Macrobiotic Summer Conference and *The Spirit of Rice* Film Documentary.

THE SPIRIT OF RICE FILM DOCUMENTARY

From left: Christian Elwell, Mark Leonas, Edward Esko, and
Naomi Esko at South River

The future of our health and wellbeing depends on our continuing relationship to our food from the ground up. As the 2020s begin, we have created
an exciting new documentary project, *The Spirit of Rice*. The film will present a compelling narrative of a central food on our planet and its key role
in shaping and influencing personal, community, and planetary health. The
film will show how to grow brown rice in your backyard or neighborhood
garden. Today, most food, including organic brown rice, is grown on an
industrial scale. This film will show how individuals and families can seed,
plant, and harvest rice on a much smaller and intimate scale in a variety
of climates and environments. The focus of the movie will be Christian

Elwell's awned rice paddy at South River Miso in Conway, Massachusetts. The film will document each stage of the rice cycle, from the preparation of seeds and planting in the spring, through to the summer flowering, the early autumn harvest, and the late autumn hand-hulling of the new crop.

Filming has already started. You can follow the progress of this project at planetaryhealth.com and *The Spirit of Rice* Facebook page. The project is being sponsored by Planetary Health, Inc., a 501(c)(3) non-profit environmental and health organization. We invite you to support this highly meaningful project with a tax-deductible donation. Donations may be made by credit card online at planetaryhealth.com or on *The Spirit of Rice Film Documentary* GoFundMe page. The documentary film is the brainchild of Sheri DeMaris, a macrobiotic teacher in Devon, PA. Sheri assembled a team of dedicated volunteers to assist with production, including Christian and Gaella Elwell, Alex Jack, Mark Leonas, Brian Smith, Alice Fava, and Naomi Esko. The film is being produced by Marlee Snyder. Contact Sheri DeMaris at teawithsheri@aol.com for more information about the project.

Made in the USA
Columbia, SC
02 October 2021